For Dion

Contents

Introduction

THE ROOT
OF IT ALL

"WE CANNOT LIVE WITHOUT THE MASS."

Any good Catholic might say that. But how many of us mean it literally? Would we really rather die than miss Sunday Mass?

For most of us it's an abstract question. But it's not abstract everywhere in the world, and it hasn't been abstract at every point in history. Right now there are Christians who choose to risk death for the sake of Sunday Mass. And in the early centuries of Christianity, the risk of death was always there. At any moment the persecution could flare up again, and Christians could be rounded up and taken off to be thrown to the beasts.

Why would they rather die than miss the Mass?

I hope you'll know the answer by the end of this book. And I hope you'll begin to feel the same way those early Christians did. I don't expect that any of us will have to be martyrs for the sake of a Sunday Mass. But we can still learn to see the world the way they saw it. We can understand that every good thing in our lives has its roots in the Mass. All our work, all our play, and all our love.

♆

IT WAS THE LAST PERSECUTION—AND THE WORST.

Diocletian was emperor, and he didn't start out with any plan for persecuting anyone. All he wanted to do was restore the Roman Empire after years of civil war and precipitous decline.

But he did want everybody to get with the program. He wanted everyone to be a good and loyal Roman. He wanted to see the ancient Roman virtues revived, and one of the main virtues was discipline. (Diocletian had been a soldier all his life.) Discipline meant that people couldn't just go off and do their own thing all the time.

And that was where the Christians were troublesome, because they were definitely doing their own thing. What was worse was that they were persuading so many other people to do it with them. Christians weren't a majority yet, but they were rapidly headed in that direction. In an empire that was a religious shopping mall, Christians were the largest single group. There was a big and prosperous Christian church practically right across the street from Diocletian's own palace.

And Christians wouldn't lay their differences aside and sacrifice to the pagan gods when everyone else was falling in line. Only the Jews had the special privilege of avoiding the sacrifices.

Diocletian had a soldier's superstition, and it was easy to convince him that the gods would be annoyed if he didn't crack down on these Christians who defied them. So he outlawed their assemblies and required them to make a sacrifice to the pagan gods. And why not? How hard can it be to toss a few grains of incense toward a fire?

But the Christians wouldn't do it. And they wouldn't stop meeting, even when Diocletian's goons burned down their churches.

So the roundups began. Soldiers descended on known Christian meeting places and scooped up all the Christians they could find.

Some of the Christians gave in. All you had to do was make the sacrifice, after all, and you could walk free. And the Romans were serious about persuading you. They were experts at painful and bloody tortures.

But in spite of the tortures, many Christians stubbornly refused to give up their faith.

That was what happened when forty-nine of them were rounded up in the town of Abitinae in Africa. They had met for the Eucharist on Sunday, in direct defiance of the emperor's decree. They refused to promise not to do it again. In fact, they continued openly defiant. So the prosecutor brought out the claws.

Roman prosecutors had a little more leeway than modern American ones. They were allowed some enhanced interrogation techniques that could be very effective. The claws were a favorite tool: sharp metal hooks used to rip open the side of a recalcitrant defendant. They were usually quite persuasive.

And yet the Christian prisoners defied even the claws.

One of the prisoners—his name was Saturninus, and he was the local Christian priest—had already seen several of his companions ripped by the claws. Yet when the proconsul berated him for defying the emperor's orders, Saturninus brazenly admitted that they had been celebrating the Lord's Supper.

"Why?" the proconsul demanded.

Saturninus's response has become a famous Latin catchphrase in the Church:

"Sine domenico non possumus."

We usually translate it as "We cannot live without the Mass." But the original statement sounds much more like something a nervous but defiant Christian might say when he's confronted by the whole might of provincial Roman authority. A closer translation would be something like "Without the Lord's thing we just . . . can't."

We just can't. We can't go on. We can't get through the week. We have no power to continue. We *need* this Eucharist, more than we need food or water. More than we need life.

And the martyrs of Abitinae were very serious about that. It would have been easy for them to say, "Oh, all right, we won't do it again." They would probably have been free to go. Diocletian wanted to crush Christianity, not kill Christians, and in the usual Roman manner his governors made it very easy for the Christians to do the sensible thing and give up their weird religion.

But without the Mass, the Abitinian martyrs just. . . couldn't. Without the Mass they just wouldn't be themselves. Without the Mass they wouldn't *be*.

One of Saturninus's companions added by way of explanation to the prosecutor: "Christians make the Mass and the Mass makes the Christians, and one cannot exist without the other."[1]

The Mass makes Christians—that's what this book is about. The Eucharistic liturgy isn't just a nice little ceremony we made up to remember a historical event, like fireworks on the Fourth of July. The Mass makes our lives whole. All the useful work we do is bound up in it. All our playful joy comes out of it. And all our Christian love funnels through it.

When Irenaeus of Lyons was refuting Christian heretics who thought that the world was created, not by the Father, but by an inferior being, he asked how they could possibly offer the Eucharist if they really thought God hadn't created the good things they offered. The Eucharist, he said, was the only argument he needed. "Our way of thinking is attuned to the Eucharist, and the Eucharist confirms our way of thinking."[2]

1   Hamman, *The Mass*, 16.
2   *Against the Heresies* IV.18.5, as quoted in CCC 1327.

Everything is measured against the Eucharist. This meal we share is what forms us as Christians.

Even more than that, the Eucharist has formed the whole world as we know it today.

CULTURE BEGINS AT THE BANQUET TABLE. In every religion, at every time in human history, shared feasts have formed—or deformed—the culture.

Sharing a meal is the most basic and most binding form of social interaction. Who can eat with whom and when? The question is almost an obsession for many cultures, because eating together means communion. If we eat together, it means that we are part of the same community.

And if we eat together with God, it means God is also part of our community.

A religious feast brings us together as people of one faith. It's the most important thing that happens to us. It takes us out of our ordinary daily routine of trying to survive and makes us part of something bigger and more important.

In fact, the British historian Christopher Dawson believed that culture must invariably have its roots in religion. He said, "From the beginning the social way of life which is culture has been deliberately ordered and directed in accordance with the higher laws of life which are religion." And again, "Throughout the greater part of mankind's history, in all ages and states of society, religion has been the great central unifying force in culture." To sum up, he made a bold statement: "Religion is the key of history."[3]

Dawson's position is usually summed up in one catchy phrase: Culture arises from cult. Our customs and habits proceed from our acts of worship.

Think of the Passover feast in Israel. Everyone in the entire community was participating in the same feast at once. And the feast was a reminder of what they had been through as a community—what had *made* them a community.

> You shall eat no leavened bread with it; seven days you shall eat it with unleavened bread, the bread of afflic-tion—for you came out of the land of Egypt in hurried flight—that all the days of your life you may remember the day when you came out of the land of Egypt.
> (Deuteronomy 16:3)

All it meant to be an Israelite was bound up in that feast. It was a reminder that the people had been oppressed, but God sent Moses to lead them out of oppression. It was a reminder that Moses had left them God's law, a law that set them apart from all the other nations of the earth. In the Passover, Israel lived through its birth again. The Mishnah, the collection of the oral traditions from the Second Temple period, makes it explicit. "In each and every

3 Dawson, *Religion and Culture*, 37.

generation one is obligated to see himself as if he went out of Egypt,"[4] the tradition says. When you celebrated the Passover, you were going through the Exodus with your ancestors.

The Passover *formed* Israel. It made Israelites out of twelve ragged tribes of nomads. Israel was Israel because the people celebrated the Passover.

And we could say the same of the pagan feasts. It was those shared meals that made pagan society what it was. It was very different from Jewish society, of course—and that was because the meals were very different.

JUVENAL, ONE OF ROME'S SHARPEST SATIRISTS, was as sharp as he ever got when he described the upper-class banquets of his day. The great English playwright William Congreve translated one of his satires into memorable English verse:

> Let him who does on iv'ry tables dine,
> Whose marble floors with drunken spawlings shine;
> Let him lascivious songs and dances have:
> Which, or to see, or hear, the lewdest slave,
> The vilest prostitute in all the stews,
> With bashful indignation would refuse.

4   *m. Pesach* 10.1–9, quoted in Smith, *From Symposium to Eucharist*, 148.

But fortune, there, extenuates the crime;
what's vice in me, is only mirth in him:
the fruits which murder, cards, or dice afford,
A Vestal ravish'd, or a matron whor'd,
Are laudable diversions in a lord.[5]

By the time of the early Christians (Juvenal was writing not long after the last books of the New Testament were finished), an upper-class banquet anywhere in the Roman world was a drunken orgy. That was what was expected. Granted, Juvenal was a satirist. He probably exaggerated the details a bit (and Congreve added a layer of exaggeration, too). But satire works because everyone recognizes the caricature.

Pagan temples often had banquets, just as we have in church social halls today. But many of those pagan feasts were orgies, too. In fact, in some of the pagan religions, the orgy was the point of it.

Among the educated classes, a common sort of banquet was the symposium, or drinking party, which was an event with religious roots and a strong sense of ritual—but also one where people tended to get completely sloshed. It was very bad manners *not* to get sloshed. Part of the ritual was to appoint one participant to be the *symposiarch*, the ruler of the drinking. He would tell people when they had to take another drink, and he would not tolerate sobriety.

5   Juvenal, Satire 11, translated by William Congreve.

There was always more than just drinking at a symposium. There might be party games—the sort where each turn somehow involved taking another drink. There might be amateur theatrical performances.

Or you might have a symposium where philosophical discussion was the main entertainment on the agenda. A particular topic would be introduced, and everyone would contribute his most sparkling thoughts on the subject. The drinking helped, of course. Everyone who's ever had a philosophical discussion while drunk can testify that brilliant ideas were flying all night. If only we could remember them the next morning. . . .

Plato's dialogue called the *Symposium* describes just such a drinking party, where the topic under discussion is love. Of course, if you invite Socrates to your drinking party, you're probably already going to have some memorable conversation. But even in Plato's carefully orchestrated little comedy, where the participants begin by intending to drink just a little, the drunkenness gets a bit out of hand.

Regardless of the agenda for the party, of course, there was music to set the mood. Every symposium worth calling a symposium had a flute-girl for entertainment. It was impossible to imagine the pagan banquet without her. These flute-girls had a reputation as something like prostitutes with added musical talent.[6]

---

6   Smith, *From Symposium to Eucharist*, 35.

And sometimes, when the flute-girl got thoroughly sloshed, the music was not the main attraction.

> The drunken flute-girl bursts our eardrums with her sodden cheeks.
> Often she has a double pipe; often just the one.[7]

That's another famous satirist, Martial, complaining about the racket the flute-girl makes when she's as drunk as the guests. Plainly she isn't there primarily for her musical abilities.

As for the guests, they might come from several classes. The upper classes usually supported hangers-on who were not quite as fortunate, but who might be clever or politically useful. Those poor clients would be invited to the banquets for their entertainment value, to add to the wit of the conversation, or just to reflect luster on the host.

But that didn't mean they had to be treated the same way the *good* guests were treated. Seating was carefully arranged according to the importance of each guest, and the worst thing that could happen to a host was to make a mistake in the seating chart. The lower class of people at the banquet might not even be eating the same food. In fact it was common for the host to dole out the food according to status. Martial complains that the better class of guest gets a fattened turtle-dove, while he gets a magpie that died in its cage. It must have seemed like an insult to

7   Martial, *Epigrams* XIV.64 (new translation).

him. But of course his host was worried that he would seem to be insulting his important guests if he fed them the same fare as the common rabble.[8]

So even when the classes came together to eat together, the class distinctions were kept up very carefully. You wouldn't want to have the lower classes thinking they were just as good as the upper classes. It was enough of a privilege that they were invited to share the dining room with their betters.

Meanwhile, the lower classes who weren't invited were having their own drunken parties to celebrate every holy day.

Once again, the meal formed the culture. The meal has been carefully arranged to reinforce what the culture has decided is important. When you went to a pagan banquet, you learned the rules of pagan society by living them. The meal told you who and what you were.

CHRISTIANS WERE DIFFERENT. They didn't make class distinctions. Or at least they shouldn't. But Paul found that his Corinthian friends were formed too much by the culture around them. They had started dragging that pagan culture into the Church.

This is the key to a passage that puzzles many readers in one of Paul's letters. Writing to the Corinthians, Paul criticizes them for emphasizing their differences

8   Smith, *From Symposium to Eucharist*, 45.

when they come together for what is supposed to be their own sacred meal.

> When you meet together, it is not the Lord's supper that you eat. For in eating, each one goes ahead with his own meal, and one is hungry and another is drunk. What! Do you not have houses to eat and drink in? Or do you despise the church of God and humiliate those who have nothing? What shall I say to you? Shall I commend you in this? No, I will not.
>
> (1 Corinthians 11:20–22)

It strikes modern readers as very strange that the Corinthians are eating different dinners at the same table. But now we know that it wouldn't have seemed odd in those days at all. That was what people did. The rich were better than the poor, so they ate better even at the same party.

Paul has to explain that this is not what Christian feasts are to be like. So he tells the story of the original Lord's Supper—the story we hear at every Mass.

> For I received from the Lord what I also delivered to you, that the Lord Jesus on the night when he was betrayed took bread, and when he had given thanks, he broke it, and said, "This is my body which is for you. Do this in remembrance of me."
>
> In the same way also the cup, after supper, saying, "This cup is the new covenant in my blood. Do this, as often as you drink it, in remembrance of me."

> For as often as you eat this bread and drink the cup,
> you proclaim the Lord's death until he comes.
>
> (1 Corinthians 11:23–26)

We hear this "institution narrative" out of context so often that we can forget what brought it up. It comes up because the Corinthians are celebrating the Eucharist like a pagan banquet. They're making class distinctions. They're stuffing their faces. They're getting drunk. And Paul has to remind them that *our* feast isn't about all that.

Our Christian feast is what makes us one Christian Church. It forms us. And if we're humiliating the poor, then it's not Christian at all. It's *de*forming us, in fact. That's why Paul is so insistent with the Corinthians: "When you meet together, it is not the Lord's supper that you eat." The Lord's Supper isn't about humiliating the poor. In the Kingdom, "many that are first shall be last, and the last first" (Mark 10:31).

This was how Jesus lived his life. In fact, the disciple who occupied the place of most honor at the Last Supper was the youngest—John, who "was lying close to the breast of Jesus" (John 13:23). That meant he was on his host's right, which was the position of highest status.

From what Paul writes we can gather that, so far, the Eucharist was still a full meal, like the Last Supper. Shortly after that, the Eucharist was separated from the church dinner—the *agape* feast. It may be that the apostles originally thought they were going to have sacred feasts the way the Jews had, and then found that the Greeks couldn't be bent to that. They had had too much experience with banquets the Greek way. If you sat them down at the table with a big feast in front of them, they were going to start acting as if they were at a typical Greek banquet. All the drunkenness and the class distinctions would come out.

That may be why Paul was having so much trouble with the Christians in Corinth. They just couldn't get the idea that the world was turned upside down when they became Christians. The pagan feasts had built their ways of thinking. These people had been formed by the meals they had shared.

But at the same time, Paul knew his friends couldn't just cut themselves off from all society. He himself was a tradesman: he supported himself with a skilled profession, and he needed customers. For that he needed to build relationships. And his customers would doubtless end up inviting him to dinner once in a while. Could you do business in a big Greek city without going to dinner? Probably not.

By the time of the early Church, the dining room was the center of everything. It was where business deals were made. It was where marriages were arranged (whether the young lady liked it or not). It was where all the backdoor political wheeling and dealing was done.

And all this had a religious undertone to it that was always made explicit in libations to the gods during the banquet. Even without the explicit offerings to the gods, if there was meat, it had probably come from a pagan sacrifice. The gods required constant sacrifices, and most of that meat ended up in the public market. In the city (and Christians were disproportionately city-dwellers in the early years), there probably wasn't any meat available that hadn't been sacrificed to some god or other.[9]

Paul recognized that the business of the world was largely conducted at the dinner table, and some of the most detailed instructions he gave his Corinthian correspondents were about how to navigate the minefields of pagan worship that were planted all through the ordinary dinners the Christians might be invited to by their neighbors. Having told them to avoid the worship of idols, he felt compelled to explain how that applied to eating together.

> I speak as to sensible men; judge for yourselves what I say. The cup of blessing which we bless, is it not a participation in the blood of Christ? The bread which we break, is it not a participation in the body of Christ? Because there is one bread, we who are many are one body, for we all partake of the one bread. Consider the people of Israel; are not those who eat the sacrifices partners in the altar?
>
> (1 Corinthians 10:15–18)

9   Smith, *From Symposium to Eucharist*, 32.

If you participate in the Eucharist, then you are making yourself part of the community of Christians. If you participate in the Jewish sacrifices, you are making yourself part of the community of Israel. And if you participate in the meal as a sacrifice to the pagan gods, then you are making yourself part of the community of the pagans.

> What do I imply then? That food offered to idols is anything, or that an idol is anything? No, I imply that what pagans sacrifice they offer to demons and not to God. I do not want you to be partners with demons. You cannot drink the cup of the Lord and the cup of demons. You cannot partake of the table of the Lord and the table of demons. Shall we provoke the Lord to jealousy? Are we stronger than he? (1 Corinthians 10:19–22)

If the Christian feast gives you communion with Christ, then the pagan feasts give you communion with the demons.

Nevertheless, Paul's main concern is not about the demons, but about the impression Christians make on their pagan neighbors. We have to remember that each one of us is a walking billboard for the true Way. It's true that we're freed from the law of Moses. But that just means we have to do some thinking on our own. What do our neighbors think of us when we eat with them? Do they think we believe in their gods? We can't leave them with that impression. We have to correct it—not for our sake, but for theirs.

> "All things are lawful," but not all things are helpful. "All things are lawful," but not all things build up. Let no one seek his own good, but the good of his neighbor.
> (1 Corinthians 10:23)

So how do you get along in a world where every bit of meat has probably been offered to some pagan god? You'll have to exercise a bit of common sense.

> Eat whatever is sold in the meat market without raising any question on the ground of conscience. For "the earth is the Lord's, and everything in it." If one of the unbelievers invites you to dinner and you are disposed to go, eat whatever is set before you without raising any question on the ground of conscience. (But if some one says to you, "This has been offered in sacrifice," then out of consideration for the man who informed you, and for conscience' sake—I mean his conscience, not yours—do not eat it.) For why should my liberty be determined by another man's scruples? If I partake with thankfulness, why am I denounced because of that for which I give thanks? So, whether you eat or drink, or whatever you do, do all to the glory of God. Give no offense to Jews or to Greeks or to the church of God, just as I try to please all men in everything I do, not seeking my own advantage, but that of many, that they may be saved.
> (1 Corinthians 10:15–33)

Not only do the feasts form you, but the way you behave at the feasts forms the people around you. You have to take responsibility for your part of the collective culture.

Especially if it's your job to change the culture.

That's why Paul was so concerned with exactly what the Corinthians were doing at dinner. At a time when books were luxuries, most people's ideas of the world were formed through the experiences they had through their lives. Religious feasts were big experiences. The pagan feasts made pagans: they taught people to think in a certain way. The Jewish feasts made Jews: they reinforced, over and over, what made the Jews different from other people. And the Christian feasts made Christians. From the liturgy they learned what it meant to be a Christian. They learned how the world was supposed to work. As one scholar of the liturgy put it, the Christian feasts "impressed the chief mysteries of faith upon the popular consciousness."[10]

And, as Paul pointed out, how a Christian behaves at other people's meals tells those other people what sort of person a Christian is.

How Christians behave at their own meals tells the Christians what sort of people they are themselves.

And they're going to need a strong idea of how a Christian behaves in the real world, because a Christian's worship doesn't end at the temple gate,

10 Jungmann, *Handing on the Faith*, 17.

the way it did if you were worshiping Apollo or Aesculapius. For a Christian, the religious ceremony is only the beginning. It's the Christian's life's work to take the love of Christ out into the world of every day.

Chapter 1

WORK

I<small>T'S NEARLY TIME FOR</small> M<small>ASS</small>, and here come bushels of cherries and peaches. And big baskets of cheese. Christians from all over the countryside are bringing the fruits of their labor to the bishop. It's almost as if they're *proud* that they worked for these things.

And they're going to be acknowledged as part of the liturgy. Everyone will know that these people worked with their hands, maybe even got dirty.

Let everyone hasten to take to the bishop, at all times, the first fruit of the fruits, and the first of the produce.

And the bishop shall also receive them with thanksgiving, and name the name of him who brought them in to him, saying,

"We give thanks to you, Lord God, and we present to you the first fruit of the fruits that you have given us, to partake of them, which you have perfected by your word; and you have commanded the earth to produce every fruit for use, and for joy, and food for the human race and for all creation. We bless you, God, for these, and all other things by which you have benefited us.

You have adorned all creation with the various fruits, through your holy Son, Jesus Christ our Lord. The glory that is through him be to you, and to him, and to the Holy Spirit for ever and ever. Amen."

These are the fruits that shall be blessed: the vine, the fig, the pomegranate, the olive, the prune, the apple, the peach, the cherry, and the almond.

But they shall not bless the garlic, nor the onion, nor the melon, nor the cucumber, nor the melon cucumber, nor the immature date, nor any other thing of the pot-herbs.

It shall be that they shall offer flowers: let them offer a rose, and the lily. But the rest they shall not offer.

But everything which they shall eat they shall give thanks to God for. And when they shall taste them they shall give glory to him.[11]

These liturgical rubrics come from a Coptic manuscript found in Egypt. But we find these same instructions almost identically worded in every common language of the Mediterranean world. All over the Roman Empire, and beyond its borders as well, people who worked in the vineyards and orchards and fields were bringing the best of their produce to the church.

The *best* is key here. That's why there's a list of things *not* to bring. The people are to bring their best to the altar, not the cheapest vegetables they can find. But

11 Coptic version of the *Apostolic Constitutions*, 53–54, translated by Henry Tattam, altered.

everything they eat is a gift of God, and they ought to remember that every time they eat. And they also ought to remember to be thankful for their fellow workers who toil to produce the food that they eat. The rubrics make it explicit that the bishop is to pronounce the name of each person bringing gifts, so everyone will know that *this* person did that work.

And that was one of the biggest revolutions in the Christian way of thinking. Because in the Roman world of the first few centuries, doing work was definitely not something to be proud of.

THE SCRIPTURES MAKE CLEAR that God made us to work, and we won't find fulfillment apart from our labors. In the very first pages of the Bible we learn that man was made in the divine image. But our God is a worker, not a layabout. "And on the seventh day God finished his work which he had done, and he rested on the seventh day from all his work which he had done. So God blessed the seventh day and hallowed it, because on it God rested from all his work which he had done in creation" (Genesis 2:2–3). God worked six days, and didn't rest until he'd got a whole universe finished.

So the Bible tells us that human beings were also made to work. We were told to "fill the earth and subdue it; and have dominion over the fish of the sea and over the birds of the air and over every living thing that moves upon the earth" (Genesis 1:28). Those are divine actions, and we were made to share them. And they're *work*. We were created to be doing something.

More specifically, in this chapter, we learn that the Lord God placed man "in the garden of Eden to till it and keep it" (2:15). The garden didn't just take care of itself. We were supposed to take care of it.

We were created, in God's image, with work as an elemental part of our nature. All of this happened before there was any talk of testing, or disobedience, or the consequences of sin. In the earthly paradise, long before there was sin, there was work. And it was good.

In fact it was more than good. Work, in the beginning, was holy. We see this in the way the story is told. Adam is commanded to "till" the garden and "keep" it. Some translations say he must work it and guard it. The original Hebrew verbs are *abodah* and *shamar*, which are elsewhere in the Hebrew Scriptures used to describe the work of priests as they tended the sacred rites of the tabernacle.

With his creation, Adam is given a task, and that task is priestly.

Well, the work of a priest is to offer sacrifice. That's what Melchizedek did. That's what Aaron did. That's what Zechariah did. That's what all priests do. So what was the stuff of Adam's sacrifice? What was he offering when there was no altar upon the earth?

It seems that the entirety of the earth was his offering, and all his work was the act of sacrifice. As

God equipped Adam for the task of subduing the earth, he was also ordaining him for priestly service.

That moment, I believe, is the true "big bang" in any Christian understanding of work. The event remains like background radiation through all the rest of salvation history, informing the way labor and laborers are portrayed in the religion of Israel—and how they're protected and regulated in Israel's law.

The background radiation is evident also in the terminology used for the priestly cult. We see in the book of Exodus that it is described simply as "service"—using the same term employed to describe the slave labor done for Pharaoh. This implies that there was an ordinariness to the tasks of the priests. But it also suggests that there was something sacred about the tasks of brickmakers, bricklayers, and quarrymen.

Greek-speaking Jews preserved this linguistic connection as they denoted their sacred rites by the word *leitourgia*—public work. We still keep the fire going today, whether we use that word's English descendant, *liturgy*, or we translate it into something more serviceable, like *service*.

We were made for work, and God intended our work to be holy.

That doesn't mean it will be easy. After Adam sins, God confronts him with the consequences of his actions, and most of them affect his work:

Cursed is the ground because of you; in toil you shall eat of it all the days of your life; thorns and thistles it shall bring forth to you; and you shall eat the plants of the field. In the sweat of your face you shall eat bread till you return to the ground. (Genesis 3:17–19)

Note that work is not a punishment for sin. Nor is it a consequence of sin. Because of our sin, however, work is burdensome to us. It can be troublesome and frustrating. But, from the beginning, it is good. It is holy. It is our sacrifice.

But that wasn't the way pagan Greeks and Romans saw it. Not at all. If there was one thing a good pagan intellectual thought would utterly ruin your chances for holiness, it was *work*.

CHRISTIANITY WAS HARDLY A HUNDRED YEARS OLD when a pagan intellectual named Celsus launched a vigorous attack against it.

This religion couldn't be true, he argued, because it was made up of shoemakers, cleaners, weavers, and other common laborers. Its God was a carpenter, for heaven's sake. His mother spun cloth. And his great spokesman was a tentmaker. How could a religion made up of such lowly people be anything but contemptible?

Celsus, assuming the person of a Jew, represents him as speaking to Jesus, and reprehending him for many things. And in the first place he reproaches him with feigning that he was born of a virgin; and says, that to his disgrace he was born in a Judaic village from a poor Jewess, who obtained the means of subsistence by manual labor. . . .[12]

We also may see in their own houses, woolweavers, shoemakers, fullers, and the most illiterate and rustic men, who dare not say any thing in the presence of more elderly and wiser fathers of families; but when they meet with children apart from their parents, and certain stupid women with them, then they discuss something of a wonderful nature; such as that it is not proper to pay attention to parents and preceptors, but that they should be persuaded by them.[13]

Woolweavers! Shoemakers! What kind of religion is this? Their God's mother was a seamstress!

Of course Celsus didn't *know* that Mary was a spinner, any more than he *knew* that she was actually pregnant by a Roman soldier named Panthera (a stock stage-comedy name for a Roman soldier). But he repeated these popular slanders precisely because he thought they gave him the edge in the debate.

12 Origen, Contra Celsum I.28, in *Arguments of Celsus, Porphyry, and the Emperor Julian, Against the Christians*, 5.
13 Origen, *Contra Celsum* III.55, in *Arguments of Celsus, Porphyry, and the Emperor Julian, Against the Christians*, 20.

And with his kind of audience, they probably did. He was speaking to upper-class gentlemen. All he had to do to make Christianity contemptible was to make them believe it was a religion of people who *worked* for a living.

Celsus believed what every gentleman of the Greco-Roman world believed: that it was base and ignoble to do useful work with your hands. That was for poor people, and they were a different species. Poor laborers (often slaves) did the work, so that rich intellectuals like Celsus had time to sit around and think intellectual thoughts.

The French social historian Paul Veyne speaks of "the ancients' contempt for labor, their undisguised scorn for those who work with their hands, their exaltation of leisure as the sine qua non of a 'liberal' life, the only life worthy of a man. . . . Not only was the worker regarded as a social inferior; he was base, ignoble."[14]

And Veyne's observation was hardly new. In the nineteenth century his countryman, the evangelical historian Charles Schmidt, remarked that work was "regarded as a hindrance to public life." It "was despised as servile, degrading to man, making him incapable of virtue, and blunting his intelligence. It was the lot of the slave."[15]

---

14 Veyne, "The Roman Empire," in *A History of Private Life*, Vol. I, 118.
15 Schmidt, *The Social Results of Early Christianity*, 63.

And it's true. Aristotle, who had studied with Plato, disagreed with his old master about a lot of things and was never shy about saying so. But he had the same instinctive disgust for the idea of manual labor. In fact Aristotle's contempt for work and workers, Schmidt observed, is foundational to his "philosophic theory of social morality."

"There are labors," the Philosopher decreed, "with which a freeman cannot be occupied without degrading himself. Such are those which particularly require bodily strength; but for these labors nature has created a special class of men. These special beings are those whom we subjugate, in order that they may take bodily labor in our stead, under the names of slaves or mercenaries."[16]

Elsewhere in the same book Aristotle considered the question of what the proper virtue of a citizen was, and concluded that people who work with their hands can't have it.

> And indeed the best-regulated states will not permit a mechanic to be a citizen. But if it *is* allowed them, we cannot then attribute the virtue we have described to every citizen or freeman, but only those who are disengaged from servile offices. . . . For it is impossible for one who lives the life of a mechanic or hired servant to acquire the practice of virtue.[17]

16 Aristotle, *Politics* VII.8; quoted in Schmidt, *The Social Results of Early Christianity*, 64.
17 Aristotle, *Politics* III.5, translated by John Gillies, altered.

Again, Aristotle is hardly alone in this. We have already heard from Celsus. Xenophon fondly recalls Socrates heaping scorn upon shoemakers, shopkeepers, and tentmakers. When his friend Charmidas confessed to being bashful about speaking in the assembly, Socrates asked him, "After all, Charmidas, who are the people you are most afraid of?—Is it the masons, the shoemakers, the fullers, the laborers, the retailers? Yet *these* are the men who compose our assemblies!"[18]

Why would you be afraid of men like those, Charmidas? When you think of it that way, it's absurd to be bashful about speaking in the assembly. Most of those people *work* for a living!

And more than half a millennium later, Plotinus held fast to the old orthodoxy. "The mass of manual laborers," he observed, "is a contemptible mob, whose purpose is to produce objects needed by men of virtue."[19]

To the most refined men of the Greco-Roman world, leisure was a virtue—and work was its opposite. It was vicious. It was a vice.

YET CHRISTIANS NEVER LOOKED AT WORK THAT WAY. Celsus was right. The churches *were* full of laborers, and they worshiped a Laborer. And their liturgy celebrated

18 Xenophon, *Memoirs of Socrates* III.7, translated by Sarah Fielding.
19 Veyne, *A History of Private Life*, Vol.1, 121.

their labors, made them holy, made them part of their offering to their God.

In fact, the Christians' scriptures preserved not the syllogisms of philosophers, but the stories of people who got work done. Abel was a herdsman. Jacob leaned into a plow. Noah was a sailor. Peter and Andrew and James and John were fishermen. Even David, the greatest king of Israel, started out as a shepherd. And Paul was one of those odious tentmakers scorned by Socrates.

There Paul was, still working hard as a tentmaker while he carried the Gospel from city to city. He reminded the Thessalonians that he hadn't been a burden to them. That was an example to them: they should work to pay their own way.

> For you yourselves know how you ought to imitate us; we were not idle when we were with you, we did not eat any one's bread without paying, but with toil and labor we worked night and day, that we might not burden any of you. It was not because we have not that right, but to give you in our conduct an example to imitate. For even when we were with you, we gave you this command: If any one will not work, let him not eat. For we hear that some of you are living in idleness, mere busybodies, not doing any work. Now such persons we command and exhort in the Lord Jesus Christ to do their work in quietness and to earn their own living.
>
> (2 Thessalonians 3:7–12)

"If any one will not work, let him not eat." This was not the creed of a Greek or Roman intellectual. *Other* people worked so that the upper-class intellectual could eat. That was what other people were *for*.

But the Christians in the beginning weren't upper-class intellectuals. Most of them weren't anyway. Most of them were men and women who got dirty and sweaty every day. And so the tradition-minded Greeks and Romans could dismiss them as ignoble.

As it happens, we know a lot about what Paul's work-day was like, because there's been a lot of careful archaeological work in Corinth. Jerome Murphy-O'Connor, a specialist in archaeology of New Testament times, has gathered the available evidence and made a vivid picture for us.

Paul certainly wouldn't have struck the average aristocrat in the street as one of the upper classes. He wasn't a shopkeeper; he was working for shopkeepers—in Corinth, for his friends Prisca and Aquila—which would put him even below shopkeepers in social class. And shopkeepers weren't very high up there in society.

There was a brand-new market square when Paul came to Corinth—the latest shopping mall, so to speak. The stores were tiny: about thirteen feet deep, and the *large* ones were thirteen feet wide. The smaller ones were only about nine feet wide. In other words, the larger stores were smaller than the average suburban bedroom in America.

Upstairs—or up ladder—was the living quarters for the shopkeeper and his family, however large that family might be. It would be the same size as the shop below, so that the whole family would be crammed into one tiny room whenever they were at home. But not a hired man, like Paul: he'd have to sleep downstairs in the shop. Prisca and Aquila would at least have some family time to themselves.

During the day there wouldn't have been much family time. Even if no one needed a tent today, the shop was in the middle of the crowd as long as the market was open.

We don't know Paul's exact address in Corinth, of course. But markets were similar all around the Mediterranean. The ones in Corinth have been well excavated and studied, and so have the ones in Ostia (the seaport for the city of Rome) and many other places. The sizes and conditions are about the same. And wherever there were markets, there were crowds.

That was probably a big advantage to Paul. When business was a little slow, he could step out onto the crowded square or street and instantly start up a conversation. He probably became an expert at those one-on-one street encounters.

Soon enough the little workshop of Prisca and Aquila had become the cathedral of Corinth. It didn't look much like what we think of as a cathedral. The small (but growing) group of worshipers would crowd into the shop after hours and sit on whatever piles of canvas or leather they could find. Archaeologist Murphy-O'Connor estimates that fifteen people at most could crowd into the little stall. It wasn't exactly a grand basilica—but it was the place where something new and exciting was happening, and more and more people wanted to be part of it.[20]

Many of those people were shopkeepers or workers like Prisca and Aquila and Paul. They heard something new in this Way that Paul was preaching: a message that they really mattered. Not only was it *all right* that they worked for a living: it was a *good thing*. Work was good. It was a gift from God—a God who, as they were reminded every time they came for worship, had become a carpenter for them.

THE IDEA THAT ORDINARY LABOR HAD TREMENDOUS DIGNITY —the idea that ordinary work could be something divine—set Christians apart from their neighbors. It was one of those crazy Christian ideas that scandalized the pagan world all around them, like the idea of a crucified God, or of the finite containing the infinite. It was something that was flung at the Christians as an insult: you people *work* for a living.

And yet Christians seemed to revel in every insult. Writing around the year 150, Justin Martyr comes out of his corner like a boxer, leading with his chin, as he heralds Jesus as the unremarkable carpenter.

20 Jerome Murphy-O'Connor, *St. Paul's Corinth*, 194–96.

And when Jesus came to the Jordan, he was considered to be the son of Joseph the carpenter. He appeared with "no comeliness," as the Scriptures declared [see Isaiah 53:2] and he was deemed a carpenter. For he was in the habit of working as a carpenter when among men, making plows and yokes. In this way he taught the symbols of righteousness and an active life.[21]

Jesus was teaching us the symbols of righteousness and an active life by *working with his hands*. That's an idea that changed the world.

Later Fathers did not hesitate to portray Jesus working at other trades, working beside Christians of their own time. A generation after Justin, in the last years of the second century, Clement of Alexandria wrote the great hymn that cast Jesus as a "tamer of wild horses."

Wherever you were working, the Church seemed to say, Jesus was working with you. Indeed, he was working within you and through you. It was a disgrace among the Christians *not* to be working, which turned pagan ideas of the good life on their head. The *Apostolic Constitutions*, speaking in the voice of the original Twelve, advises everyone to have a job.

Let the young persons of the Church try to minister diligently in all necessaries: mind your business with all becoming seriousness, so that you may always have enough to support yourselves and those that are needy,

---

21 Justin, *Dialogue with Trypho* 88 (ANCL, altered).

and not burden the Church of God. For we ourselves, besides our attention to the word of the Gospel, do not neglect our inferior employments. For some of us are fishermen, some tentmakers, some husbandmen, so that in this way we may never be idle. . . . Labor continually, therefore, for there is no healing the blot of the slothful. But "if any one will not work, let him not eat" among you. For the Lord our God hates the slothful. For not one of those who are dedicated to God ought to be idle.[22]

If you're a Christian, you're supposed to be working. Sloth is a sin!

In fact, Clement had to warn his flock in Alexandria—a city with a lot of rich people in it—that they shouldn't be treating the *rich* with too much contempt. He wrote a whole treatise called "Who Is the Rich Man Who Shall Be Saved?" The message was that it's *possible* for the rich to be good Christians. Of course, the rich do have a lot to overcome. Of course, people who flatter the rich are godless and treacherous, puffing them up to their doom. But isn't it possible for a real Christian to be a true friend to the rich?

Instead of basely flattering the rich and praising them for what is bad, it seems to me that it is far kinder to help them in working out their salvation in every possible way—asking their salvation of God, who surely and sweetly bestows such things on his own children, and

---

22 *Apostolic Constitutions* II.63 (ANF, altered).

> thus by the grace of the Savior healing their souls, enlightening them and leading them to the attainment of the truth.[23]

We should do what we can for the rich, who have so many disadvantages, so that they can be saved along with the poor. And we certainly shouldn't insult them just because they're rich.

> Those, then, who are actuated by a love of the truth and love of their brethren, and neither are rudely insolent towards those of the rich who are called, nor, on the other hand, cringe to them for their own avaricious ends, must first by the word relieve them of their groundless despair, and show with the appropriate explanation of the oracles of the Lord that the inheritance of the kingdom of heaven is not quite cut off from them if they obey the commandments. . . .[24]

Not *quite* cut off. Granted, it's hard to be rich, but you can still make it.

"Clement implies that the rich had a kind of second-class status among the Alexandrian Christians," as the scholar Annewies van den Hoek points out.[25] Clement wouldn't have had to warn his flock about mistreating the rich if he hadn't seen it happen.

23 Clement of Alexandria, *Who Is the Rich Man That Shall Be Saved?* I (ANF, altered.)
24 Clement of Alexandria, *Who Is the Rich Man That Shall Be Saved?* III (ANF, altered.)
25 Van den Hoekr, "Widening the Eye of the Needle: Wealth and Poverty in the Works of Clement of Alexandria," in Holdman (editor), *Wealth and Poverty in Early Church and Society.*

Again, this was a radical notion. The gods of antiquity were projections of the upper classes, and the myths were narratives of the mischief of a leisured life. In pagan mythology, Zeus, the chief of the Greek and Roman gods, had at least a hundred lovers in addition to his wife Hera, and had children with all of them. Many of them came to bad ends when he abandoned them without a backward glance. He set the tone for the rest of the pantheon.

And the pantheon seemed to set the tone for the upper classes. Adultery was the Roman national sport. Abandonment and death was the usual fate of the children produced by it.

Even the practice of religion itself tended to favor the rich. The mystery cults were open almost exclusively to the leisured classes (and sometimes the military). You needed time and money to rehearse the doctrines and undergo the rites.

Yet the Christian God was himself a carpenter, whose Father in heaven was always toiling away. Jesus told his opponents, "My Father is working still, and I am working" (John 5:17).

The Christian preachers who trained new converts gave them a countercultural message. Clement of Alexandria reminded new converts that there was no need for them to quit their jobs—or even to dream of doing so: "Tend to your farming if you're a farmer; but know God while you labor in the fields. Sail if navigation is your profession, but always invoke the celestial pilot. Was it in a military career that the knowledge of God first came to you? Well, then, obey the Commander who orders you to do just things."[26]

And such preaching was effective. It worked, and it converted people in every walk of life. Clement's contemporary, Tertullian of Carthage, boasted of the Church's explosive growth. "We are but of yesterday, and we have filled every place among you! Cities, islands, fortresses, towns, marketplaces, the very camp, tribes, companies, palace, senate, forum—we have left nothing to you but the temples of your gods."[27]

It wasn't just preaching that made this happen. Once you were a baptized Christian, the mystery of the Eucharist became part of your life. In every liturgy, *your own work* was celebrated. We saw that earlier in that liturgy from the *Apostolic Constitutions*. When you brought forward the first fruits of your labors, the bishop announced *your name* in front of the whole assembly. Here's someone who did good work for us, the congregation heard.

The message that work was good wasn't just an occasional sermon topic. It was woven into the *liturgy*—a word that itself meant "work." You couldn't worship as a Christian without taking that message away with you. The scholar Carl A. Volz suggests that everything Christians did in their lives was rooted in that liturgical celebration.

26 Clement of Alexandra, *Exhortation to the Greeks*, 10.
27 Tertullian, *Apology* 37 (ANCL, altered).

> We are all familiar with the famous dictum of Prosper
> of Aquitaine, who in the fifth century coined the axiom,
> *lex orandi, lex credendi* ["the law of prayer is the law
> of belief"]. I propose a variation on this principle by
> suggesting *lex orandi, lex operandi*, the law of prayer
> gives birth to the law of works, and my test case will be
> the early church before Gregory the Great.[28]

His conclusion is that the liturgical practice of the
Christians was a large part of what made them live
different lives from those of their neighbors.

THE NEW CHRISTIAN FAITH led the faithful not to aban-
don their duties, but to excel in them. Again, Tertullian
made clear that this made Christianity different from
other world religions—even the religions of far-off
India, which was a place well-known to the Romans,
who were obsessed with India's pepper.

> We are called to account as harm-doers on another
> ground, and are accused of being useless in the affairs
> of life. How in the world can that be true with people who
> are living among you, eating the same food, wearing the
> same clothes, having the same habits, under the same
> necessities of existence?

28 Volz, "Lex Orandi, Lex Operandi: The Relationship of Worship
    and Work in the Early Church".

We are not Indian Brahmins or Gymnosophists, who dwell in woods and exile themselves from ordinary human life. We do not forget the debt of gratitude we owe to God our Lord and Creator; we reject no creature of his hands, though certainly we exercise restraint upon ourselves, so that we may not make immoderate or sinful use of any gift of his. So we sojourn with you in the world. We do not stay away from the forum, or the market, or the bath, or the booth, or the workshop, or the inn, or the farm fair, or any other places of commerce. We sail with you, and fight with you, and till the ground with you; and in the same way we unite with you in your traffickings. Even in the various arts we make public property of our works for your benefit.

How it is we seem useless in your ordinary business, living with you and by you as we do, I am not able to understand.[29]

We are not far into Christian history, and already we see the effects of a revolution. In the world, Christians were as ubiquitous as God; and, like their God, they were working still.

While Plato, Aristotle, and Plotinus saw "necessity" as the bane of human life, Christians like Origen, another Alexandrian, celebrated it as the engine of divine providence.

29 Tertullian, *Apology* 42 (ANCL, altered).

The lack of the necessities of human life led to the invention, on the one hand, of the art of husbandry, on the other to that of the cultivation of the vine; and also to the art of gardening and the arts of carpentry and blacksmithing, by means of which were formed the tools required for the arts that minister to the support of life. The lack of covering, again, introduced the art of weaving, which followed that of wool-carding and spinning; and again, that of house-building: and thus the intelligence of men ascended even to the art of architecture.

The lack of necessities also caused the products of other places to be conveyed to those who were without them by means of the arts of sailing and navigating. So that even on that account one might admire the Providence that made the rational being subject to need in a far higher degree than the irrational animals, and yet all with a view to his advantage.[30]

Writing in response to that pagan snob Celsus, Origen is positively exuberant about labor. He celebrates every legitimate form of work—and even treats the *need* to work as a gift of a provident, fatherly God.

By the middle 400s, when Christianity had been the official religion of the Roman Empire for a century, Pope Leo the Great could assume that his congregation knew about the dignity of work—at least in the abstract. They might still be snobs, but they knew it wasn't *right* to be snobs.

30 Origen, *Against Celsus*, IV.76 (ANCL, altered).

Let no man consider his fellow vile, nor despise in anyone that nature which the Creator of the world made his own. For can anyone who labors deny that Christ claims that labor as done for Christ himself? Your fellow-slave is helped by means of it, but it is the Lord who will repay.[31]

YET NOT EVERY LABOR WAS GOOD. In the life of a Christian, labor was part of your worship. You would take it to the altar with you every time you went to Mass. And some professions simply weren't suitable. You can't take every kind of work with you to the altar.

In fact, Christians kept lists of unsuitable professions. *The Apostolic Tradition*, a book of liturgy and church practice often attributed to Hippolytus of Rome (who was martyred in the year 235), lists a number of jobs a Christian can't continue in. You can't be a pimp, for example, or a prostitute. You can't be a gladiator or a chariot-racer. You can't be an actor (from what we know about the theater in Hippolytus's time, being an actor was not much different from being a prostitute). You can't be a pagan priest, obviously. You can't be a governor or a magistrate in the imperial government. You can't be a magician or an astrologer.

The Christians would welcome you if you practiced any of these professions. But they would say, "You have

31 Leo, Sermon 9.2 (NPNF, altered).

to give that up before you can join us. If you won't stop, you'll have to be rejected."

There were other professions that you could continue in if you were *very careful*. "If a man be a sculptor or a painter, he shall be taught not to make idols. If he will not desist, let him be rejected." This was a hard condition, since a large part of any artist's work would have been in making idols, or in making decorations that included pagan deities and mythological scenes. Occasional funerary portraits probably weren't enough to make a living. Fortunately, though, the Christian market was rapidly expanding, and a newly Christian artist might find he had all the contacts he needed in the local church for a new career making decorations for Christian houses and tombs.

"If a man teach children worldly knowledge, it is indeed well if he desist. But if he has no other trade by which to live, let him have forgiveness." The reason for this provision is that pagan mythology, as embodied in the great pagan writers of the past, was the basis of worldly education. You couldn't teach Greek without teaching Homer, for example. A Christian could make it clear that he didn't believe those pagan gods were real, but still being a teacher meant constant wallowing in paganism.

You could continue as a soldier if you swore that you would not execute anyone, even if you had to defy orders, and that you would not take the pagan military oath. But once you were a Christian you couldn't volunteer to be a soldier.[32] The dangers of sin were just too great.

The reason for all these prohibitions and careful distinctions is that, if you're Christian, your work is part of your worship. You aren't joining some cult where you just have to show up, participate in the ritual with all the right words and gestures, and walk out assuming the god is pleased. Your worship goes on twenty-four hours a day for the rest of your life.

AND THE MASS IS WHERE IT BEGINS AND ENDS. You bring your work in to offer it as part of the sacrifice of the universal Church. You leave with the spiritual strength to go back to your life of working worship. Your whole daily routine becomes a divine mission. Just by laboring *as a Christian* you're joining in the work of creation. You're filling the world with the spirit of Christ, as the Second Vatican Council told us in *Lumen Gentium ("Light of the Nations")*:

> The faithful, therefore, must learn the deepest meaning and the value of all creation, as well as its role in the harmonious praise of God. They must assist each other to live holier lives even in their daily occupations. In this way the world may be permeated by the spirit of Christ and it may more effectively fulfill its purpose in justice,

32 *The Treatise on the Apostolic Tradition of St Hippolytus of Rome, Bishop and Martyr,* edited by the Rev. Gregory Dix.

charity and peace. The laity have the principal role in the overall fulfillment of this duty. Therefore, by their competence in secular training and by their activity, elevated from within by the grace of Christ, let them vigorously contribute their effort, so that created goods may be perfected by human labor, technical skill and civic culture for the benefit of all men according to the design of the Creator and the light of His Word.[33]

But no matter how holy and dignified work is, you need more than work. You need time away from work to be fully human. Since creation, God has told us to take at least one day off out of every seven. And it wasn't just a suggestion. It was an order.

33 *Lumen Gentium* 36.

Chapter 2

PLAY

ABOUT A QUARTER-CENTURY AGO, when I was in my twenties, I was working for a fast-growing company in what was then an emerging technology. I found the work interesting and rewarding. I got regular promotions and raises. I was also a serious Catholic, though, and it kind of bothered me that I wasn't finding time for regular prayer.

So I went looking for a spiritual director, and I found my way to a priest of Opus Dei.

The name *Opus Dei* attracted me because I knew from high-school Latin that *opus* meant "work"—and I was all about my work. So I geared up to talk with him about office politics, the perils of ambition, workplace temptations, and so on. I had an agenda.

But the priest had other plans. He looked at me with the most genial smile and asked: "What kind of vacation are you planning for your family this summer?"

I figured this was small talk to ease us into the really important stuff. So I spoke vaguely about my intention to hit a state park for a long weekend.

But he kept smiling that big, genial smile as he responded, "A stone gives more."

The conversation, and my spiritual direction, had taken an unexpected turn. Before a half hour was up, I'd begun to see that leisure was not the same as laziness. It could be something holy and something integrally human.

THIS IS NOT THE WAY we usually think about leisure in modern Western society. Especially in America. We feel guilty about our leisure. Often we *are* lazy, but we feel guilty about it even when we take time off for good things. I know people who feel guilty about taking time off for Mass, because they really ought to be out there working.

Since at least the time of the Industrial Revolution, we've been almost programmed to think that only work is virtuous, and the only thing more virtuous than work is more work.

Joseph Pieper, a German philosopher of the mid-twentieth century, published a book in 1952 that became an instant classic. It was called *Leisure the Basis of Culture,* and the main point of it is right there in the title. Leisure, Pieper believed, was where culture came from, and without leisure there would literally be no culture.

In earlier times, no one would even have questioned that idea. If anything, as we saw, the ancients were *too* fond of leisure, and too ready to condemn labor as standing in the way of refinement. In fact, that was why they had to have classes of society—slaves and laborers to do the work that had to be done, so that refined gentlemen could exercise their minds at leisure.

But Pieper saw that modern industrial civilization was abandoning leisure in favor of a dogmatic attachment to work.

> In his well-known study of capitalism, Max Weber quotes the saying, that "one does not work to live; one lives to work," which nowadays no one has much difficulty in understanding: it expresses the current opinion. We even find some difficulty in grasping that it reverses the order of things and stands them on their head.[34]

Now, I don't want to give the wrong impression. I'm not trying to say that work is bad, or that work is somehow a punishment for original sin. (See chapter 1.) You'll occasionally hear that said by religious people. I remember once hearing someone say, "If the original sin had been sloth, we'd still be in paradise."

But that's not true. As we saw before, Adam and Eve had work to do from the beginning. Even God was hard at work—six days out of the week. It was good, fulfilling work, both for God and for his creatures. It wasn't a burden: it was a constant joy. We human beings were working *with* God on creation!

34 Pieper, *Leisure the Basis of Culture*, 20.

And yet God still took a day off on the seventh, and expected his creatures to do the same. No matter how much they loved their work, they had to stop for a while.

So there's something holy about work, but there's something even holier about *not* working.

IT'S TRUE THAT WE WERE "put" on earth to work the earth. We're hardwired for labor, and we won't be satisfied unless we fulfill God's command.

But that's not the end of the story. Because work itself is ordered to something greater. God's six days of "labor," his six days of creation, are ordered to a Sabbath of rest.

"And on the seventh day God finished his work which he had done, and he rested on the seventh day from all his work which he had done" (Genesis 2:2).

Now, historical critics arch an eyebrow at the line and dismiss it as anthropomorphism—the tendency of primitive peoples to project human qualities onto God. But I think the Church Fathers and early rabbis had a clearer sense of the sacred text and its sacred meaning. And they saw something else happening in that text in the book of Genesis—something far richer.

Our work is service due to God. He commanded it, and it's necessary (by his design) for the continuing creation and sanctification of the world. But work is merely preliminary, and it's secondary in importance. Our more important service is worship, and the mark of worship is *leisure*. The seventh day.

As one of the ancient rabbis put it, the Sabbath is "last in creation, first in intention."

It's all about that rest.

But let's think again about the statement in Genesis. If God is who we say he is—almighty and unchanging—he doesn't grow tired, and he never needs to rest. If he *did* "take a rest" in the biblical narrative, why did he do it?

He did it, like a good father, in order to show his children how it's done. He was modeling the leisure he wanted us to keep, and he institutionalized it in the Sabbath. It's one of the ten most important rules he gave the people of Israel.

Remember the sabbath day, to keep it holy. Six days you shall labor, and do all your work; but the seventh day is a sabbath to the LORD your God; in it you shall not do any work, you, or your son, or your daughter, your manservant, or your maidservant, or your cattle, or the sojourner who is within your gates; for in six days the LORD made heaven and earth, the sea, and all that is in them, and rested the seventh day; therefore the LORD blessed the sabbath day and hallowed it. (Exodus 20:8–11)

It's almost as if God is daring us to trust him—to let go of the plow (or the computer keyboard, or the tool chest) and rest in confidence that the Creator who started the job can finish it just fine, with or without our ten-hour days. When we rest on Sunday, when we schedule our vacation, when we make ample time to look away from the computer screen and look into the eyes of our children, we are showing God that we trust him. It's an outward sign of our innermost faith.

This was probably one of the things that seemed most suspicious about the new Christian faith to the pagan upper classes. It was upending the natural order of things by giving leisure to *workers*—even *slaves.*

When Pliny the Younger was governor of Bithynia (in the year 103), he found a plague of Christians infesting his province. And he had no idea what to do with them.

So he wrote to the emperor Trajan to ask advice. He explained that he had rounded up some people who were accused of being Christians, but these were not the sort of Christians who were interested in a glorious martyrdom. They all were willing to deny Christ and offer sacrifices to the emperor's statues. Some of them said they'd given up Christianity years ago. And anyway, what they were doing wasn't all *that* bad.

They affirmed the whole of their guilt, or their error, was, that they met on a certain stated day before it was light, and addressed themselves in a form of prayer to Christ, as to some god, binding themselves by a solemn oath, not for the purposes of any wicked design, but never to commit any fraud, theft, or adultery; never to falsify their word, nor deny a trust when they should be called upon to deliver it up: after which, it was their custom to separate, and then re-assemble, to eat in common a harmless meal. From this custom, however, they desisted after the publication of my edict, by which, according to your commands, I forbade the meeting of any assemblies. In consequence of this their declaration, I judged it the more necessary to endeavor to extort the real truth, by putting two female slaves to the torture, who were said to officiate in their religious functions; but all I could discover was, that these people were actuated by an absurd and excessive superstition.[35]

What do you do about people whose superstition is so crazy that some of their leaders are slaves? Slaves who think they have the right to . . . think? Female slaves who think they have the right to think? Slaves aren't supposed to have leisure, from which it follows that slaves aren't supposed to have happiness. Happiness is for the leisured classes, as Aristotle pointed out centuries earlier:

Besides, any person whatever, even a slave, may enjoy bodily pleasures no less than the best man; but no one allows that a slave partakes of happiness except so far as that he partakes of life.[36]

35 Pliny, Letters X.97, translated by William Melmoth.
36 Aristotle, *Nicomachean Ethics* 10.6, translated by R. W. Browne.

Trajan's answer was very moderate. Don't go looking for these Christians. Don't accept any anonymous accusations, because you know how *that* turns out—everybody with a grudge denouncing his enemy as Christian. And if your Christian repents and offers a sacrifice to the gods, then fine, he's off the hook.

But of course if you do find some Christians and they won't give it up, you're going to have to kill them.

Still the Christians wouldn't give up their Sunday Mass. Some did, of course—the ones that Pliny found who were keen to let him know that they weren't into that stuff anymore, no sir. But many more didn't. Even though it was illegal. Even though the penalty was death.

They couldn't live without the Mass. They couldn't live without that break from daily work to encounter the divine.

It was a sacrament, and it was a vacation. And the Christians understood that the vacation itself—taking time away from useful work to do something *more* than useful—was something like a sacrament.

THERE ARE, OF COURSE, BENEFITS TO VACATION in the natural order. Our bodies need rest. Our minds need rest. Even old Aristotle was a practical man, and he saw the benefits of taking some time off to amuse ourselves.

But to amuse ourselves in order that we may be serious, as Anacharsis said, seems to be right: for amusement resembles relaxation. Relaxation, therefore, is not the end, for we have recourse to it for the sake of the energy.[37]

Modern research has confirmed that employees who rest are indeed more productive than employees who work without ceasing. Aristotle was right. If you relax, you have more energy to get things done. So maybe your slaves ought to have some time off to go get drunk, because they'll be better and more productive slaves overall. At least when they sober up.

As believers, we don't deny such benefits in the natural order; but, again, we recognize that there's something more to the story.

Rabbi Abraham Joshua Heschel, in his profound little book *The Sabbath*, observed that Aristotle got things exactly backward. Heschel wrote:

> To the biblical mind . . . labor is the means toward an end, and the Sabbath as a day of rest, as a day of abstaining from toil, is not for the purpose of recovering one's lost strength and becoming fit for the forthcoming labor. The Sabbath is a day for the sake of life. . . . The Sabbath is not for the sake of the weekdays; the weekdays are for the sake of the Sabbath. It is not an interlude but the climax of living.[38]

---

37 Aristotle, *Nicomachean Ethics* 10.6, translated by R. W. Browne.
38 Heschel, *The Sabbath: Its Meaning for Modern Man*, 14.

The weekdays are for the sake of the Sabbath rest. Our work is for the sake of our leisurely worship. Everything we accomplish on Monday through Friday, we accomplish for the sake of the Lord's Day.

This truth was vividly expressed in the liturgy of the early Christians in Rome. We heard earlier about all the things they brought forward to the altar, things we still bring today—bread and wine and whatever we've gained from "passing the basket." But the people also brought forward oil, cheese, vegetables, olives, salt, milk, and honey. What a beautiful image of the "fruit of the earth . . . and work of human hands"! What a beautiful image of the very moment when our week-day work finds its Sunday fulfillment!

At the altar the priest offers all of our labors in union with the Body and Blood of Jesus Christ, and so the world is sanctified. It is made holy, because we have made our priestly offering. We know that our work is made holy by being bound up with the Eucharist. But now we look at it from the other point of view and realize that the Eucharist is *why* we do the work. That day of participation in the divine is the reason we have jobs, the reason we get on with life.

The Second Vatican Council spoke eloquently of this as it spoke of the labor—and the *priesthood*—of the laity, in which we share Christ's eternal priesthood.

For besides intimately linking them to His life and His mission, He also gives them a sharing in His priestly function of offering spiritual worship for the glory of God and the salvation of men. For this reason the laity, dedicated to Christ and anointed by the Holy Spirit, are marvelously called and wonderfully prepared so that ever more abundant fruits of the Spirit may be produced in them. For all their works, prayers and apostolic endeavors, their ordinary married and family life, their daily occupations, their physical and mental relaxation, if carried out in the Spirit, and even the hardships of life, if patiently borne—all these become "spiritual sacrifices acceptable to God through Jesus Christ" (1 Peter 2:5). Together with the offering of the Lord's body, they are most fittingly offered in the celebration of the Eucharist. Thus, as those everywhere who adore in holy activity, the laity consecrate the world itself to God.[39]

Here, on the altar, the priesthood bestowed on Adam—the priesthood Adam forfeited by his sin—is restored in Christ. So none of our work need be futile. None of our work is wasted. All of it finds fulfillment in this place where we offer the world to God in our works, as our priestly sacrifice.

As Rabbi Heschel pointed out, labor is a means to an end.

---

39 *Lumen Gentium* 34.

What we need to learn, and relearn, and relearn, is that the Mass is its ultimate end. Because we anxious providers can toil away endlessly and forget why we're toiling. "I'm doing it for my children," we protest. "My work is an expression of my love." Again, there's much truth to that, and I don't want to dampen the ardor of anyone's love.

Yet we should also keep in mind the effects of sin on all human expressions of love. To borrow a phrase from the self-help books, love can go "toxic" on us, if we let it. We can turn beautiful, God-given expressions of love, like sex and work, into self-serving addictions. We work more and more and more, not just because we want to feed the family and do God's will, but because we like the adrenaline high . . . the prestige . . . the feeling of superiority over our coworkers . . . or the brute pride in productivity.

Please don't get me wrong. I'm all for healthy competitiveness. I think the world would be a much better place if we all approached our workdays with holy ambition in overdrive. But the adjectives "healthy" and "holy" are important qualifiers.

My long-ago spiritual director was right. Our leisure is an important test of the condition of our souls.

ONCE CHRISTIANITY BECAME not only legal but the favored religion of the Roman Empire, Christians had more leisure on their hands. It was partly because there was less time spent worrying about being thrown to the beasts, and partly because there were more rich aristocrats turning to Christianity.

And what did the Christians who had leisure do with their time? It looks as if Pieper was right. They started to take what was already unique about Christian culture and build on it, until Christian culture was where everything exciting in thought and the arts was happening.

Pagan culture had long since fallen into decline. That's a polite way of saying it was *boring*. By the 300s, we see almost no interesting pagan writers. All the interesting intellectual activity was going on among the Christians.

Bishops like St. Gregory Nazianzus (who became a bishop in 372) had busy lives. But with no persecutions to worry about, they weren't just living from one emergency to another. Gregory had time to write poems, huge numbers of them. He was one of the leading poets of his day, in fact—and that was in addition to his mounds of prose works: sermons, tracts, letters, and so on.

When Gregory took up the pen to write poetry, he wrote from a completely Christian perspective. He'd been given the best education in all the pagan classics, but he turned all that education to Christian uses. In the process he—and other Christians like him—made a new kind of poetry, introspective and spiritual in a way that pagan poetry had never been.

The famous English poet Elizabeth Barrett Browning, an accomplished classical scholar, thought Gregory a fascinating poet. "He spoke grandly, as the wind does, in gusts; and as in a mighty wind, which combines unequal noises, the creaking of trees and rude swinging of doors, as well as the sublime sovereign rush along the valleys, we gather the idea from his eloquence less of music than of power. Not that he is cold as the wind is—the metaphor goes no further: Gregory cannot be cold, even by disfavor of his antithetic points. He is various in his oratory, full and rapid in allusion, briefly graphic in metaphor, equally sufficient for indignation or pathos, and gifted peradventure with a keener dagger of sarcasm than should hang in a saint's girdle."[40]

Browning translated many lines of Gregory, including his poem on "Soul and Body":

> What wilt thou possess or be?
> O my soul, I ask of thee.
> What of great, or what of small,
> Counted precious therewithal?
> Be it only rare, and want it,
> I am ready, soul, to grant it. . . .

After a long list of things his soul *might* want—power, glory, fame, and so on—Gregory comes to the startling conclusion of his first section:

40 Browning, "Some Account of the Greek Christian Poets," in *Poetical Works*, 605.

What then wouldst thou, if thy mood
Choose not these? what wilt thou be,
O my soul? a deity?
A God before the face of God,
Standing glorious in His glories,
Choral in His angels' chorus?

Go! upon thy wing arise,
Plumed by quick energies,
Mount in circles up the skies:
And I will bless thy winged passion,
Help with words thine exaltation,
And, like a bird of rapid feather,
Outlaunch thee, Soul, upon the aether.

"A God before the face of God" would certainly
startle a pagan philosopher. Striking as it is, though,
it's perfectly orthodox Christian thought. Christ
shared our nature so that we could share God's nature.

Then Gregory turns to address his flesh, which
probably wants a lot of things, but isn't going to get
them from him:

But *thou*, O fleshly nature, say,
Thou with odors from the clay,
Since thy presence I must have
As a lady with a slave,
What wouldst *thou* possess or be,
That thy breath may stay with thee?

> Nay! I owe thee nought beside,
> Though thine hands be open wide.[41]

This is a sort of internal debate new in poetry. It's not really a comic poem, but at the same time it's a playful idea: setting the soul against the body, as if they were a pair of tenants who lived inside Gregory.

Another famous poet of the time made her reputation on the back of a pagan poet. But the way she did it, once again, is uniquely playful. I'd say it's almost wacky.

Faltonia (or Falconia) Proba also lived in the 300s, the time when Christianity was already three hundred years old as a faith, but brand new as the leading religion of the Roman Empire. She was a convert to Christianity, and she decided to take up a fiendishly difficult, and very playful, poetic form and turn it to Christian uses.

The form is the *cento*, which originally meant a patchwork coat. It's a poem made up entirely of lines from other poems. The challenge is to take those lines and put them in an order that means something entirely new. It has to make sense. If it's good, it has to have its own poetic effect.

Proba took upon herself the challenge of making a cento entirely from verses of Virgil, the most famous Roman poet of all time. His story of Aeneas leaving Troy and eventually founding the Roman nation is as pagan as it can be—Roman deities are major characters,

41 Gregory Nazianzen, "Soul and Body", tranlated by E.B.
    Browning

and the whole story is about Aeneas coming to realize that he has a mission decreed by fate. Yet Proba took lines from Virgil and told the story of Adam and Eve, the Flood, and Christ.

How did she do it? She'd had a good education in the classics, obviously. She knew her Virgil upside down and inside out. But she could make Virgil into Christian history because she was even more steeped in Christianity than in the classics. And how was that? Obviously, her education had been on the traditional classical lines, reading—and memorizing—the great pagan authors of the past. But Proba had also gone to the Christian liturgy since she converted. Every time she went there, she heard the Gospel preached. And every time she went there, she lived through the events of salvation history, as they were presented again in the liturgy. The liturgy made her an eyewitness to the story of salvation. It formed her into the kind of Christian who was capable of rearranging Virgil to tell a Christian story, because the Christian story had permeated her mind through the Mass.

But what made her *want* to do it?

We could point out that Virgil was the most important writer in traditional Latin education, so that even Christian children were steeped in Virgil's *Aeneid*. They had to learn the stories of pagan gods and heroes as a fundamental part of their schooling. Even though they were being taught Christianity by their parents, their whole school curriculum was pagan. So Proba could have decided that it would be useful if she could present Christian truth in Virgil's words. The students could have the perfectly polished verses of Virgil as their models, but they would be learning the story of salvation.

That would be a good reason for starting the project. But it wouldn't keep her going till she finished it. There can really be only one reason why Proba would play such a difficult game with words: it was *fun*. It was also a challenge, like a really hard crossword puzzle. And it's a lot of work, but the satisfaction of seeing the pieces fall into place keeps you going.

In a Christian world, it was *good* to enjoy a bit of fun like that.

A cento is just about the most playful form of poetry. It's a complicated poetical joke requiring tremendous effort. We don't know how much work Proba put into hers. But when a certain Mrs. H. A. Deming from San Francisco tried playing the game in English in the 1800s, it took her a year to make up a poem out of lines from the greatest English poets—and Mrs. Deming's poem was only 33 lines.[42] Proba's cento is 694 lines.

Think of the change that had happened in the world, where a Christian *woman* was taking up a fiendishly difficult intellectual challenge like this. And Proba was only one of a large number of Christian women in the 300s who were educating themselves in ways that had been off-limits to respectable women before.

42 Dobson, *Literary Frivolities, Fancies, Follies and Frolics,* 179–81.

At any rate, Proba's cento was a big success. There were critics, then and now, who thought nothing good could come out of making a cento. (Elizabeth Barrett Browning was not kind to Proba.) But most people who read poetry in Proba's time seemed to think that Proba had succeeded in making a poem that was moving and entertaining in its own right, in addition to the impressive labor of putting it all together from bits and pieces of Virgil. Furthermore, she earned a lot more fans in the Renaissance, when people like the great Italian writer Boccaccio singled her work out for praise.

The ultimate compliment is that Proba's cento became a standard part of Christian education in many places. If her mission was to give Christian students some way to learn good classical Latin without being swamped in paganism, then mission accomplished.

Once again, we see a Christian poet who has absorbed what it means to be Christian from the liturgy and then found a way to *play* with it.

Now, I don't mean to say that there was never anything playful about pagan poetry. Pagan poetry was wonderfully diverse. But I think we see a transition in the main focus of poetry when the world started to become Christian. And it's a transition that emphasizes the joy of being alive—the joy that comes from that little taste of heaven at Sunday Mass every week.

In pagan times, the dominant form of poetry was epic. Every poet hoped to have an epic in him. Virgil wrote charming little poems about farming life, but when he buckled down and got serious he wrote the *Aeneid*—at the average rate of two lines a day, or so they say.

Just about the time of the Christianization of the world, though, we start to see a transition from the epic to the lyric—from the huge to the smaller. Epics practically disappear. And I think there might be a reason for that.

The epic is a grand attempt by the pagan poet to force the world into order. The *Aeneid* would make the world Roman, whether the world liked it or not. It was big enough to contain everything important about history and geography, and to force them all into a Roman mold.

But the Christian poet felt no such pressure. The world doesn't need to be ordered, because it already *was* ordered. Then, as now, all of history is a grand story that has a known beginning and is leading to a known happy ending. The liturgy itself expresses the order of the world perfectly: it's always the same, yet infinitely varied by local circumstance, by the calendar, and by the people celebrating it. It's a perfect expression of freedom within order.

And because Christian poets found a world that already had a grand pattern, they could concentrate on the small delights of creation.

PERHAPS THE MOST FAMOUS POET of the 300s is Ausonius, who was born in about 310, just before the Roman emperor Constantine legalized the practice of Christianity. He came from an educated family in Bordeaux (in modern France), and he had the best education their money could buy. With that education he rose high, even being made consul one year—the highest honor a citizen could aspire to.

Ausonius seems to have been a convert to Christianity. And here's where his story gets a little bit interesting, because most of his biographers think he was a lukewarm Christian, who converted just because it gave him better prospects in the imperial government. But their only evidence is that much of his poetry isn't explicitly Christian.

So here's the question. Do Christian poets always have to be writing about Christian theology? Or is enjoying the world around you a Christian thing to do?

Ausonius did enjoy the world around him. There's no question about that. And he was a sinner: there's no question about that, either. He seems to have kept a mistress. It would be nice to say that he can't have been a real Christian if he was a sinner, but we all know that's not true. Christians are sinners: that's why Christ came to us, in fact. The healthy don't need the doctor.

We can say that he was a bad Catholic, but do we have to say that he didn't really believe in his Christian religion?

It seems to me that Ausonius takes a lot of joy in the little things, and the reason his poetry isn't mostly about church or theology is because he just takes it for granted that the whole world is God's work.

One of his most famous poems is his "Ephemeris; That Is, the Business of a Whole Day." It's a delightful account of one day in the life of a Roman gentleman. Every little detail of the daily routine is worthy of Ausonius's poem, starting with getting up and calling his servant. You might think the servant would be getting the master out of bed in the morning, but that isn't the way things work in Ausonius's household. It takes a lot of effort to get that servant out of bed—one of the many amusing little details that add to the feeling that you're living his day right along with Ausonius. And once he finally manages to wake the servant, we get the impression that Ausonius feels as though he's going to be late for his appointments. Nevertheless, he has to leave time for morning prayers.

> Boy! Hey there! Get up and get
> my shoes and my muslin robe.
> Get me everything that's ready
> to wear, so I can go out.
> Get me spring water to wash
> my hands and mouth and eyes.

And get the chapel opened up—
but with no showy preparation.
Pious words, innocent vows
are plenty for our prayers.[43]

Once the chapel is ready, we hear Ausonius's prayer. It's a good one. But it's not the whole poem. Formal prayer is just part of everyday life.

I think that's the way it *should* be for a Christian whose business is in everyday life.

After his prayer, it's already close to noon (Ausonius seems to have slept in late himself, in addition to the time he spent waking up his servant), and it's time to go out and make the usual social rounds. There are invitations to be given and accepted. And then he has to come back and supervise his cook, who might not get the seasoning right without his help. Or at least that's what Ausonius thinks. And then there's time for dictating to his secretary—maybe dictating this very poem. Ausonius takes time to admire how skillfully the secretary takes down everything he says, no matter how fast he talks, on his wax tablets: it seems as though the fellow writes things down before Ausonius even says them.

When it's time for sleep, Ausonius describes his dreams and nightmares. Sometimes there are robbers or monsters. Sometimes he dreams that he's flying. Sometimes he has dreams of lust that

43 Ausonius, *Ephemeris* II (new translation).

make him feel ashamed of himself. Sometimes he sees himself at court or at the theater. He has all the dreams that everyone still has today, and he describes them as part of his life.

That's what makes this poem remarkable. It's not the deeds of a legendary hero. It's the most ordinary events of an ordinary day in an ordinary life. It's the life of a Christian gentleman who knows he's a sinner, but who's confident that God has a place for him even so.

In fact, the key to Ausonius's attitude may be his petition near the end of his morning prayer:

> Father, give me the hoped-for breath of eternal light,
> if I do not swear by stone gods, and—
> looking up to only one altar of reverend sacrifice—
> bring you the offering of an unstained life;
> if I know you as the Father of our Lord and God
> the Only-Begotten, and, joined with the two,
> the Spirit who was moving over the waves of the sea.[44]

Ausonius lives his life like an ordinary Roman gentleman—but he's a Christian gentleman. His whole life itself is his offering. In the liturgy, he brings it to the altar—the one altar for the whole world. And so every little detail of his life is part of what he offers. His morning crankiness, his round of social calls, his fussy household management, his dreams good and bad. Himself, in other words. At Mass, he brings everything that makes Ausonius Ausonius to the altar.

44 Ausonius, *Ephemeris* III (new translation).

Maybe this poem *is* all about his faith after all. It's just that the critics haven't recognized it, because they haven't recognized that Ausonius's calling is everyday life. His Christian vocation is to live the life of an ordinary Roman gentleman in a Christian way, and to bring that life, however flawed, to the altar as his offering.

Yes, you might say that he's a little arrogant for calling his life "unstained." His life isn't unstained because he's still a sinner. His life is unstained because his stains can be washed away.

Now, what use is a poem like this? Absolutely none, you might say. It serves no purpose. It doesn't put food on the table. It doesn't keep out the rain. It's just a useless bit of fun.

But from leisure comes culture, if Joseph Pieper is right. And if Christopher Dawson is right, that's because we need leisure for *cult* (see introduction). We need time to approach the divine, even if that isn't immediately useful to us.

So when Ausonius wraps his whole life up in a poem and presents it as his offering to God and God's people, he's helping to create a new kind of Christian culture—one that celebrates the everyday, even the mundane, precisely because that's where God is in a Christian's life. The Christian hero isn't someone who kills monsters and founds empires. The Christian hero is someone who has the courage to get up in the morning and live a good life. And maybe that's just as exciting and just as heroic as all that stuff about the monsters and the empires.

Critics who are used to the standards of the earlier classical age of Greek and Roman poetry don't know quite what to make of Ausonius. He was the most famous and most respected poet of his time, and the classicists can't figure out why. He gets so caught up in the *little* things. Where's the grand epic sweep? What happened to the carefully worked-out proportions of classical literature?

Christian critics, however, have been hardly kinder to Ausonius. They question his faith because his work—unlike the work of his contemporaries who were clergy—rarely concerns theology or church affairs or lives of the saints. For them a Christian poet is one who writes like a bishop or a monk. The ideal would be Paulinus of Nola, who was a monkish bishop, and who wrote long works describing pilgrim shrines. (Paulinus was also a student and frequent correspondent of Ausonius.)

Ausonius, alas, frustrates the expectations of both the classicist and the clericalist.

But if I'm right, it's the little things that matter to Ausonius—*precisely because the world has turned Christian.* A Christian world cares about little things, because not one sparrow is forgotten before God (see Luke 12:6). The little details of everyday life are heroic.

At any rate, I don't think it's coincidental that, shortly after Ausonius, we get the greatest masterpiece of autobiography of all time—Augustine's *Confessions*. Following the example of Gregory Nazianzus and Ausonius, Augustine turns his gaze in toward his inner self. Like Gregory, he looks deeply into his own soul. Like Ausonius, he remembers the humblest details of his everyday life. And out of those he builds a self-portrait so powerfully moving that it's been the model for every autobiography ever since.

I've spent all this time talking about poetry and literature because it's easier to talk about writing in writing. But things were changing in all the arts.

For example, consider painting and sculpture: Christians started out with what they inherited from the pagan world, before moving far beyond it. In fact, it can be notoriously difficult to identify an early Christian burial in an ancient painting or sculpture, because the decorations used were often the same as pagan decorations. Is a bunch of grapes a sign of the Eucharist, or is it just a decorative bunch of grapes?

But over time Christians began to develop their own distinctive art—art whose purpose was to bring the people and events of salvation history to life in the imaginations of the Christians. It wasn't an art of refined aesthetics. You could argue that it wasn't always as skillful as pagan art of the classic age. But its purpose was to communicate directly.

In music, Christians began setting their most important truths to melody almost right away. Several quotations in Paul's letters seem to be from Christian hymns that were already circulating all through the Church, so that he could just mention them and expect his audience would know what he was talking about. As the Church grew, the liturgy itself became more musical. Hymns started to be part of the celebration— catchy tunes that you could walk home singing, and that would teach you the basics of Christian theology while you sang.

Christians, in short, started spinning culture out of their leisure. The weekly day off to celebrate the Mass grew into a distinctively Christian way of looking at the world that showed up in literature, art, and music.

And it all grew out of the Mass.

OF COURSE, LEISURE ISN'T EVERYTHING. Our society is obsessed with work, but there are some who err in the opposite direction. They care too much about leisure—the lazy kind of leisure that's all about bodily pleasure and has nothing to do with building culture.

You may, if you are old enough, remember the band Loverboy's hit single from 1981: "Everybody's Working for the Weekend." Some people do pass their weeks for the sake of the freedom to party on Friday and Saturday and sleep in on Sunday. Some people do work overtime for months just to afford a freewheeling, drunken week aboard a cruise ship. Such party animals are really as far as the workaholic from the true experience of Sabbath rest.

This is why I think Ausonius had it right, and the critics who doubt his sincere Christianity have it wrong. In leisure we take delight in creation—in the simple good things of life. And we do it not just because it makes us feel good, but because it gives glory to God. On Sunday, for example, we enjoy the company of spouse and children and grandchildren, not simply because that's what's on the schedule for Sunday, but because we have freed our minds to see these people as they are, and see them for what they are.

As Christians we have the custom and obligation to worship on Sunday, and our great and obligatory act of worship is called the Eucharist for a reason. The name, remember, comes from the Greek *eucharistia*, which means "thanksgiving."

When we attend a Sunday liturgy with our families, we have a God-given chance to *stop*—to hit the pause button on all our arguments and frustrations—and see a spouse, a child, a parent, a grandchild as a gift from God. And we have a chance to thank God for the gift.

God doesn't *need* our thanks, and he doesn't *need* our worship. If he has commanded these actions, it is because he knows *we* need them. He knows they're good for us.

Worship should be, for our families, a *sine qua non* (most essential thing) of every Sunday. It should also be an important component in our vacations.

Now hear me out. I'm not saying we should vacation like nuns. (Unless you're a nun, in which case you really should.) Vacation needn't feel like a novena to our kids. But we should take pains to avoid excursions to places where it will be impossible or extremely arduous to get to worship on Sundays or holy days. We should also make sure not to schedule activities that will crowd out our church attendance. Today we have access to great databases that will direct us to the nearest churches and chapels.

We should also do the research and find vacation spots that will not compromise our morals. Some ski lodges, for example, and some beaches have a better moral atmosphere than others. Same goes for amusement parks. It helps to ask more experienced Christian parents and grandparents. They're usually happy to answer when you ask them about their happiest vacations.

And if you have the discipline to live it in a leisurely way, consider a "staycation"—an extended time when you and the family can take day trips to local attractions. You may have to put a little effort into planning it. Leisure, paradoxically, requires work on our part, a little planning, a little expense. But the effort, too, is labor for the sake of a Sabbath. We toil now so that we can relax for a while and let God work in our leisure and through our leisure.

To leave work on time, to forego the optional Sunday shift, to use vacation time rather than piling it up—these are acts of trust. And they are tithes we pay to God, simple and small tokens acknowledging that he is really the owner of all our hours of all our days.

I come back to the great philosopher Josef Pieper, who after all wrote the book on Leisure—as Rabbi Heschel wrote the book on the Sabbath. Pieper noted that the biblical phrase usually translated as "Be still, and know that I am God" (Psalm 46:10) can also be translated "Have leisure, and know that I am God."

The leisure God wants us to have is not the absence of activity. It's rather a different kind of activity. It's not just vegetating on the couch. No. It's freedom.

It's freedom to be receptive to what the Jesuit Gerard Manley Hopkins called "the dearest freshness deep down things."[45]

Leisure is an opportunity to draw close to God, in himself and in others, in relaxed study and in prayer, in delight in his creation and in the delightful contingency of a shared ride on the roller coaster.

Leisure is a notoriously unproductive thing, when judged by industrial standards, but it does produce such moments, and such moments are holy.

And in leisure, in the spirit of the Sabbath, come works of a different sort: poetry, music, art.

From the undistracted gaze comes the strongest family bond.

From hymns sung in refreshment the Church is renewed.

45 Hopkins, "God's Grandeur."

As St. Augustine put it, *"Cantare amantis est"*[46]—singing is for lovers. Christians sing because love overflows in song. It's not useful at all—not unless it's useful to make the world just a little bit better every day. Then maybe Christian joy is useful after all. Because Christian joy overflows in Christian love.

And when that happens, the world really does change.

---

46 St. Augustine of Hippo, Sermon 336,1.

Chapter 3

LOVE

NORTH AFRICA, IN THE YEAR 190: PEOPLE ARE BEGINNING to wonder why there seem to be so many Christians all over the place.

Christianity was still fairly new on the world scene. It had begun just a few generations before in a remote Roman province called Judea, located at the edge of the Roman Empire, and it was just beginning to reach important African cities like Carthage (in what is now Tunisia). The Christian religion was so new and unusual that it baffled people and required an explanation.

So a prominent lawyer named Tertullian, a convert to Christianity from Roman polytheism whom we met already in chapter 1, offered the explanation he thought the pagans around him needed. He wrote an *Apology* that still stands as a model defense of Christian life. He was an early practitioner of what we now call apologetics.

As you probably know, an *apology* in philosophy doesn't mean saying you're sorry. Not at all. It means a defense—the sort of defense a lawyer would make in front of a judge. Tertullian's *Apology* addressed in particular the elements of Christianity that his pagan neighbors found revolutionary, threatening, alarming, or just plain strange and different.

What non-Christians found so different about Christianity was not so much its rituals, or its books, or the architecture of its temples. It was not its clothing, or dietary restrictions, or monuments, or art. It was its kindness. The most notable feature of Christian life was the charity and unity of Christian believers. This is how Tertullian explained it:

> We have our treasury, but it's not made up of admission fees, as in a religion that may be bought. Once a month, each person puts in a small donation, but only if he wants to, and only if he can. There is no compulsion. Everything is voluntary. These gifts, then . . . are not taken and spent on parties, drinking binges, and restaurants, but to support and bury poor people, to supply the wants of orphans, and elderly people who are homebound, those who have suffered shipwreck, and those who have been condemned to work in the mines, or banished to the islands, or shut up in prisons. . . . It is such deeds of noble love that lead many to put a brand upon us and say, "See how they love one another!"[47]

Charity, peace, unity, kindness: these were the most striking qualities of Christian life, as seen from the outside. And the Church's way of life was so different,

47 Tertullian, *Apology* 39 (ANF, altered).

so distinctive, that it was like a brand mark or tattoo on the Christians' bodies. Their love was visible. You couldn't miss it.

The citizens of Carthage who worshiped the Roman gods knew little or nothing about the Church's sacraments and doctrines. Those were private affairs, conducted behind closed doors. The local pagans knew little about Christianity's inner life—but they knew the city's Christians by their way of loving one another, which was evident for all to see. Love is what set Christians apart from their non-Christian neighbors, even as it attracted those same neighbors to Christianity.

This was not a quality unique to the African church. It was a quality the African Christians held in common with believers in Rome, Antioch, Alexandria, and Gaul. This was what people noticed about the Christians. Even before Tertullian, St. Justin Martyr gave the same testimony for the Church in Rome.

> And those who are well to do and willing give what each thinks fit; and what is collected is deposited with the president, who helps the orphans and widows and those who, through sickness or any other cause, are in want, and those who are in bonds and the strangers sojourning among us, and in a word takes care of all who are in need.[48]

48 Justin Martyr, *First Apology*, 67 (ANF, altered).

These words come from the middle 100s. We often quote Justin's description of the charity of the very early Roman church to show how, even as a poor underground cult, the Church took care of the needy.

But if we just quote those words, we miss a big part of the point. We miss the context. The fact is that Justin is only *incidentally* describing Christian charity. It comes up while he's describing the Christian liturgy— the most detailed description we have of that liturgy at such an early stage in the Church's history. And what he's telling his pagan audience is that the Christians' worship involves helping the poor as a necessary part of the ritual. It's not just a nice thing they do, like some benevolent society (not that there were many benevolent societies in the Roman world). Charity *is* worship, and worship flows into acts of charity.

It's not that taking care of the people who needed it wasn't important. It's just that the Mass was so much *more* important. The Mass was *supremely* important. The Mass was where people learned to love like Jesus—and where they received the strength to love like Jesus.

That's why it's important to remember the context when Justin tells us how the Christians support the poor. Here's more of the context. First Justin describes in detail exactly what the Eucharist is, and what we believe about it—that it's the Body and Blood of our Savior. Then he goes on to describe the Christians' Sunday meetings:

And on the day called Sunday, all who live in cities or in the country gather together to one place, and the memoirs of the apostles or the writings of the prophets are read, as long as time permits; then, when the reader has ceased, the president verbally instructs, and exhorts to the imitation of these good things.

Then we all rise together and pray, and (as I said before), when our prayer is ended, bread and wine and water are brought, and the president in the same way offers prayers and thanksgivings, according to his ability, and the people assent, saying Amen. And there is a distribution to each, and a participation of that over which thanks have been given, and to those who are absent a portion is sent by the deacons. *And those who are well to do and willing give what each thinks fit; and what is collected is deposited with the president, who helps the orphans and widows and those who, through sickness or any other cause, are in want, and those who are in bonds and the strangers sojourning among us, and in a word takes care of all who are in need.*[49]

Justin was a philosopher, as everyone could tell. He chose to wear the uniform. It was an advertisement for the philosophy business: a professional philosopher made his living by taking on students, so it helped that people could recognize a philosopher right away. More than that, though, it was a status thing. Philosophers were proud of their intellectual

49 Justin Martyr, *First Apology,* 67 (ANF, altered).

accomplishments, and they liked it when people recognized them.

Aulus Gellius was an exact contemporary of Justin Martyr; they lived in Rome at the same time, and could have run into each other on the street. He tells a story about an indigent philosopher that perfectly illustrates what it meant to Justin to be wearing a philosopher's robes:

> In my presence, a certain man, with a long cloak and hair, and with a beard reaching to his girdle, approached Herodes Atticus, a man of consular rank, eminent for his amiable disposition, and his accomplishments in Grecian eloquence, and requested money to be given him for bread. Herodes on this asked him who he was? He, with an angry tone and frowning countenance, replied, he was a philosopher; and expressed his surprise that he should be asked who he was, when his appearance declared it.[50]

Of course Herodes was teasing the man; he knew the man was supposed to be a philosopher, but in fact he turned out to be a vile and contemptible fellow who hung out in the brothels and wore the uniform to go begging.

For Justin, the philosopher's uniform had an even more important meaning than status or advertisement— although Justin did take on students, and the advertisement was probably important. His philosopher's

50 Aulus Gellius, *Attic Nights*, IX.2, translated by the Rev. W. Beloe.

uniform said something about his Christian faith. This is a real philosophy, it said. It's not just for ignorant servants and poor sailors. You need to take it seriously.

At the same time, however, when he describes what's really distinctive about the Christians, it isn't so much what they think. It's what they do, because what they do shows their love. And this Christian love flows out of their Sunday worship. It's been that way since the time of Paul.

Like every preacher since then, Paul had to deal with the offering question. Preachers would rather be preaching about almost anything else, but the subject of contributions will come up, because the Church stops working if the people don't contribute.

So when he had to bring up the subject with the congregation in Corinth, Paul first gave them the inspiring example of the Macedonians.

> We want you to know, brethren, about the grace of God which has been shown in the churches of Macedonia, for in a severe test of affliction, their abundance of joy and their extreme poverty have overflowed in a wealth of liberality on their part. For they gave according to their means, as I can testify, and beyond their means, of their own free will, begging us earnestly for the favor of taking part in the relief of the saints—and this, not as we expected, but first they gave themselves to the Lord and to us by the will of God.
>
> (2 Corinthians 8:1–5)

First they gave themselves to the Lord. For Paul, charity begins with worship. And the worship leads inevitably to the charity.

Justin was a philosopher, but this was something new, something not dreamt of in Aristotle's philosophy.

THERE REALLY WAS NOTHING like Christian charity in the pagan world. Pagan religion was never about what *you* could do for *other* people. It was about what the gods could do for *you*. It was about getting the gods on your side, or at least not having them against you. The whole Greek and Roman system of worship taught and reinforced selfishness.

But what about the great philosophers of the pagan world—Plato, Aristotle, and the like? Surely they had something more than selfishness to offer. They were all about living the good life. And that included dealing with other people. Didn't Aristotle say that man was a political animal—meaning an animal that lived in a *polis*, a city?

Yes, Plato and Aristotle both acknowledged that the human condition was social. But most of what they said about virtue was about what the virtuous man (Aristotle wouldn't have considered the possibility of a virtuous *woman*) had to do to build up his own virtue, and what advantage that was to him. Again, the virtue was self-centered. It was just a more refined version of the pagan ideal that the virtuous man is the one who gets what he wants out of life and doesn't have to worry much about other people. In fact, the virtuous man in pagan philosophers generally gets along without other people as much as possible. Those philosophers had learned their early lessons too well from the pagan worship all around them.

The Christians looked at the pagan philosophers and saw thinkers who *tried* to get it, but lacked the one essential thing. They were missing love.

> For God, since he is kind, wished us to be a social animal. We do not deserve to be rescued from our own dangers if we do not help others; we do not deserve assistance if we refuse to render it. The philosophers have no precepts of this sort. Captivated by false virtue, they have taken away mercy from humankind. They want to heal vices, but they have increased them instead. And though they generally admit that people will still have to deal with each other in human society, they entirely separate themselves from it by the harshness of their inhuman virtue.[51]

That was how the Christian writer Lactantius described what was wrong with pagan philosophy. Lactantius was a philosopher himself: he was a professor of rhetoric, meaning that he had to know

---

51 Lactantius, *Institutes* VI.10 (ANCL, altered; I took the alternate reading *dum volunt sanare vitia, auxerunt*).

his pagan classics backwards and forwards. And he was exceptionally good at his trade: he had become an advisor to the emperor Diocletian, but he became a Christian and luckily resigned his position before the big purges of Christians began. Later he became one of Constantine's chief advisors. So Lactantius was someone who had a right to his opinions on pagan philosophers.

But it's not just Lactantius. Anyone in the Christian era who reads the pagan philosophers is struck by how essentially self-centered they are. And in that they simply reflected the whole world around them, built on the most basic assumptions they had learned from their religion. The nineteenth-century German historian Gerhard Uhlhorn puts it very bluntly right at the beginning of one of his books:

> Our Lord calls the commandment of love which He gave to His disciples a new commandment (John 13:34). And such indeed it was, for the world before Christ came was a world without love.[52]

How can he say that? After all, the Greeks had three different words for three different kinds of love, as every Bible expositor is fond of pointing out.

But what Uhlhorn means is that there was no sense that loving your neighbor—whether he seemed lovable or not—was something you *ought* to do. There was none of what we call *charity*. There were beggars,

52 Uhlhorn, *Christian Charity in the Ancient Church*, 3.

so obviously some people felt pity and gave to the poor in an individual and unorganized way. But there wasn't a program of organized charity. That would have to wait for the Christian revolution.

That's something we can't easily wrap our minds around today. Before Christianity, the Greco-Roman world knew nothing like institutional charities. Before Christianity, there were no hospitals. Before Christianity, there was no drive for universal education, or world peace. Before Christianity, there was no serious discussion of the ethics of warfare. No trade schools. No programs for the destitute.

There was wealth and there was poverty, each condition dependent upon the existence of the other.

In fact, although some individuals felt a twinge and gave to a beggar, the wise Greek or Roman would probably tell you to leave the beggar to starve. In one of Plautus's comedies, the young playboy Lysiteles sees an old friend who's been reduced to begging. He wants to give the man something, but his father, Philto, gives him stern advice.

Philto. You deserve to be insulted by a beggar if you give him something to eat or drink. You yourself lose what you give, and you extend the beggar's life for more misery.

Lysiteles. I'd be ashamed to desert him and not help when things are rough for him.

Philto. Hmph! It's better to be ashamed now than annoyed later. They've got the same number of letters.[53]

Now, Christians didn't have to ask whether you should give something to a beggar. "Give to him who begs from you, and do not refuse him who would borrow from you" (Matthew 5:42). That was what the Lord said, and it was a simple principle to follow. The earliest Christians followed it in their own congregation: "And all who believed were together and had all things in common; and they sold their possessions and goods and distributed them to all, as any had need" (Acts 2:44–45).

Material goods were only temporary, after all. As it says in the Letter of Barnabas, a very old Christian writing that was sometimes included in early New Testament collections: "You will share in everything with your neighbor, and do not say that things are yours. For if you are sharing in what is indestructible, how much more in the destructible!"[54]

You are the people who have *everything*. What are material goods in comparison with what you have as Christians?

---

53 Plautus, *Trinummus*, Act 2, Scene 2 (new translation). In Latin, the words for "ashamed" and "annoyed" are *pudere* and *pigere*, which also have the same number of letters.
54 Barnabas 19:8 (new translation).

Pagan philosophers might have agreed that material goods should be regarded as worthless. But for them that meant that the wise and virtuous man should have a healthy contempt for material goods, so that if he happened to be deprived of them, he wouldn't suffer much. It didn't mean that filthy beggars should have his material goods.

But what if the beggar doesn't deserve our gifts? What if he's a fake? Another very popular early Christian book, the *Shepherd of Hermas*, had an answer for that, too.

> Do good work, and out of your toil that God gives you, give freely to anyone who is deprived, not asking whether you will give to someone or not. Give to all, for to all God wishes gifts to be given out of his own gifts.[55]

Hermas goes on to explain that the person receiving the gift is responsible for whether he deserves it or not. That's not your concern. You just respond to the need.

RESPONDING TO NEED wasn't something educated pagans thought about much.

They did have an idea of *philanthropy*. They had a word for that, after all. But philanthropy was, paradoxically, a very self-centered thing.

---

55 Shepherd of Hermas 27:4 (new translation).

If you go to Rome and look at the Pantheon, the best-preserved of all the pre-Christian buildings in the city, you'll notice right away that it was donated by Marcus Agrippa. You'll notice it because it says so in billboard-size letters right across the front of the temple.

Rich people were expected to spread their wealth around that way. They gave games, for example, where ordinary people could watch gladiators kill each other or watch criminals (like Christians) get gobbled up by beasts. These spectacles cost huge amounts of money, and there was always a race on to see who could spend *more* money and give the people *more* spectacle. Or they built public baths, which would carry the name of the donor.

That was the point of philanthropy. It was to make people notice the donor, usually so that his political career would go well. So naturally what he gave had to be something big and spectacular. It wouldn't occur to a Roman philanthropist to fund medical care for lepers, for example. You can't write your name in big letters on a leper.

Now contrast the way the world was organized when the Christians began to have some organizing power. Right away we see the difference between *philanthropy* and *charity*.

We've already seen that, even when the Church was a persecuted underground fledgling religion, the bishops organized charity. The offering was part of the liturgy. Those offerings had to go somewhere, and the bishop was responsible for making sure they went to people who needed them.

As the Church grew, the bishops had more and more resources at their disposal. In Alexandria, for example, the Christians had an ambulance brigade that went out into the streets looking for people who needed help. The Alexandrian church organized its charity on a large scale, and dedicated employees worked to relieve the suffering around them.

The most ambitious program was the one established by St. Basil of Caesarea in Cappadocia (now the city of Kayseri in Turkey). History knows him as Basil the Great—for very good reasons.

Basil lived at a time when the Arian heresy had the ear of the emperors, so it was a constant struggle just to be an orthodox bishop. And Basil joined in the theological debates with a rare talent for careful distinctions. But he still found time to take care of the poor in his home city. And there were a lot of poor. There were widows who had no one to take care of them. There were sick people who had no money for doctors. There were travelers who had run out of luck and had nowhere to go. There were old men who couldn't work anymore. There were children with no parents. Worst off of all were the lepers, victims of a wasting skin disease that deformed them hideously and made them social outcasts.

Many other Christians saw the poor and sick and did what they could, helping one at a time. Some bishops, like the bishops of Alexandria, organized their charitable works. But Basil looked at the problem and saw that it was gigantic.

Then in the year 369, there was a famine. Suddenly the problem was more than a problem: it was an emergency. That gave Basil the excuse he might already have been looking for, the excuse to start tackling the problems of human misery in a truly organized way. He immediately started up a food bank or soup kitchen where people who couldn't pay the inflated prices for food could be fed. And once he got started, Basil didn't stop. He began to tackle all the other problems he saw around him—the lepers, the widows, the orphans, the homeless.

In the suburbs of Caesarea, Basil began putting up institutions that would be able to accommodate large numbers of people who needed help. He had an orphanage, a hostel for poor travelers, a hospital, a retirement home, a homeless shelter, a vocational school, a leprosy sanitarium—whoever needed help could find it. There were so many buildings that the place began to look like another city. People called it the Basiliad—Basil's Place.

In fact there were a few grumblers who didn't like the idea of the local bishop taking so much responsibility into his own hands. Remember that the Arian controversy was in full swing. The Arian party didn't like to see an orthodox bishop succeeding this way. Basil found that he had been reported to Elias, the provincial governor, as a person to keep an eye on.

So he wrote his own defense in a letter to the governor that still survives—along with well over three hundred of Basil's other letters. (Somehow he found time to be a prolific writer in addition to everything else.)

Now I should like those who are besieging your impartial ears to be asked, What harm does the government suffer from me? What loss is suffered by any public interests, small or great, by my administration of the churches?

All right, it might possibly be urged that I have done damage to the government by erecting a magnificently appointed church to God, and around it a dwelling house, one liberally assigned to the bishop, and others underneath, allotted to the officers of the church in order—which you of the magistracy and your escort are welcome to use.

But to whom do we do any harm by building a place of entertainment for strangers, both for those who are on a journey and for those who require medical treatment on account of sickness, and so establishing a means of giving these men the comfort they want—physicians, doctors, means of conveyance, and escort? All these men must learn such occupations as are necessary to life and have been found essential to a respectable career; they must also have buildings suitable for their employments, all of which are an honor to the place, and, since their reputation is credited to our governor, confer glory on him.[56]

Notice the politically astute turn Basil gives the argument: these are improvements in *your* jurisdiction, so they add to *your* reputation. Won't everybody think you're a fine governor when they see how well you take care of the poor and sick?

Note also the details Basil mentions in passing. The place was run like a big business. It was remarkable for its size, but also for being professionally staffed. There were real paid physicians in the hospital, not just a few monks with some first-aid training. And medical care was very good in those days. There wasn't modern technology, but the standards of hygiene were high, and surgery was very sophisticated. The poor would be getting the best medical care money could buy. There seem to have been ambulances, too, and there was job training for people who needed work.

When Basil died, this complex of charitable institutions stood as his monument. His lifelong friend Gregory Nazianzus—we remember him as the talented poet—wrote a eulogy for Basil, in which the Basiliad came as the climax of the story.

---

56 Basil, Letter 94, To Elias, Governor of the Province (NPNF, altered).

Go out a little way from the city, and behold the new city, the storehouse of piety, the common treasury of the wealthy, in which the superfluities of their wealth—yes, and even their necessaries—are stored, in consequence of Basil's exhortations, freed from the power of the moth (see Matthew 6:19), no longer gladdening the eyes of the thief, and escaping both the emulation of envy, and the corruption of time: where disease is regarded in a religious light, and disaster is thought a blessing, and sympathy is put to the test.

That was how Gregory described Basil's foundation. Gregory thought this was a more marvelous thing than any of the seven wonders of the world.

Why should I compare with this work Thebes of the seven portals, and the Egyptian Thebes, and the walls of Babylon, and the Carian tomb of Mausolus, and the Pyramids, and the immeasurable weight of bronze of the Colossus, or the size and beauty of shrines that are no more, and all the other objects of men's wonder, and historic record, from which their founders gained no advantage, except a little bit of fame? My subject is the most wonderful of all, the short road to salvation, the easiest ascent to heaven.

Gregory dwells especially on the plight of the lepers, because they were the ones most people wouldn't touch with a ten-foot pole. Basil took the lead in caring for lepers with his own hands, and made other people ashamed not to follow his example.

There is no longer before our eyes that terrible and piteous spectacle of men who are living corpses, the greater part of whose limbs have mortified, driven away from their cities and homes and public places and fountains—yes, and from their own dearest ones—recognizable by their names rather than by their features: they are no longer brought before us at our gatherings and meetings, in our common intercourse and union, no longer the objects of hatred, instead of pity on account of their disease; composers of piteous songs, if any of them have their voice still left to them. Why should I try to express in tragic style all our experiences, when no language can be adequate to their hard lot?

But it was Basil who took the lead in pressing upon those who were men, that they ought not to despise their fellow men, nor to dishonor Christ, the one Head of all, by their inhuman treatment of them; but to use the misfortunes of others as an opportunity of firmly establishing their own lot, and to lend to God that mercy of which they stand in need at his hands. He did not therefore disdain to honor with his lips this disease, noble and of noble ancestry and brilliant reputation though he was, but saluted them as brethren, not, as some might suppose, from vainglory (for who was so far removed from this feeling?) but taking the lead in approaching to tend them, as a consequence of his philosophy, and so giving not only a speaking, but also a silent, instruction. The effect produced is to be seen not only in the city, but in the country and beyond, and even the leaders of society have vied with one another in their philanthropy and magnanimity towards them.

Others have had their cooks, and splendid tables, and the devices and dainties of confectioners, and exquisite carriages, and soft, flowing robes; Basil's care was for the sick, and the relief of their wounds, and the imitation of Christ, by cleansing leprosy, not by a word, but in deed.[57]

Of course the point of this eulogy is to praise Basil, and his friend Gregory does a good job of that. But think of how many other people had to be involved. The place was staffed with monks and nuns, of course: people who devoted their lives to this one mission of bringing Christ's love to the poorest of the poor. And the people of Caesarea had to fork over a lot of money to keep up the place. Buildings mushrooming in the suburbs: that sort of thing doesn't pay for itself. And that brings us right back to the liturgy, because all this public work of the Church flowed out of the *primary* public work of the Church—the Mass.

That was where the people brought their gifts. That was where those gifts became part of the offering of the Church. And that was where Basil preached. No doubt people were encouraged to give generously by some of Basil's sermons.

57 Gregory Nazianzen, Oration XLIII, 63 (NPNF, altered).

Secular histories of the hospital trace the whole *idea* of the hospital in the Western world to Basil's Basiliad, the "new city" devoted to making Christian love work on an industrial scale. As the medical historian Thomas Heyne notes, Basil's institutional charity soon found many imitators. "It seems that Basil started a new trend: soon after his death, similar Christian hospitals were sprouting up elsewhere in the Roman empire, and they became commonplace within one century."[58]

But wait. There was one major speed bump on the road to a Christian world in Basil's lifetime. There was one emperor who thought he could erase everything the Christians had accomplished in half a century of being out of the closet. He hated Christians and wanted to bring back the rapidly fading pagan religion of the already ancient Greeks. Yet, in some ways, he was one of the most Christian emperors Rome ever had.

I ALWAYS TELL THE STORY of Julian the Apostate when I'm talking about the Christian revolution, because nothing shows us better how quick and how thorough that revolution was.

58 Thomas Heyne, "Reconstructing the World's First Hospital: the Basiliad," in *Hektoen International: A Journal of Medial Humanities.*

Julian was born in a Christian family. Unfortunately his family was a family of emperors: his grandfather was Constantius Chlorus, the father of Constantine. When Julian was young, his cousin Constantius II became emperor, and he celebrated by massacring almost all his male relatives. Julian and his older brother were just little boys at the time, and Constantius spared them—either out of pity or, more likely, because he couldn't see how they would be a threat. Julian was raised in a gilded cage, given a Christian upbringing, but educated in the standard way—which meant that he had a pagan tutor who taught him the great literature of the pagan past.

To all appearances Julian was a good Christian as a young man. But when he found himself sole emperor of the Roman Empire in the year 360, he suddenly declared that he had just been kidding. He was really a pagan, and he was going to return the Roman Empire to its pagan glory.

It didn't work, of course. For one thing, Julian died only a year and a half later, killed in battle against the Persians. For another thing, Christianity had sunk in too deep to be rooted out. And the best proof of that is Julian himself.

In order to bring back paganism to its former glory, Julian had to pick up the ruined pieces of the pagan cults. In fact there had never been a thing that was paganism: there was only a variety of cults of various deities, all of them tolerating each other but operating independently. Julian couldn't imagine how that would work. Having appointed himself the pagan pope, he set about making a pagan church on the centralized-and-distributed model of the Christian Church. One of his letters to his pagan archbishop in Galatia survives, in which he explains that pagans will have to out-Christian the Christians if they want to get anywhere. After congratulating himself on how well his pagan revival is going (a little wishful thinking there), Julian goes on to explain that the pagans are going to have to be a lot more like the wicked Galileans, as he liked to call the Christians.

> But why should we be satisfied with this, and not instead pay attention to the means by which this impiety [he means Christianity] has increased—namely, humanity to strangers, care in burying the dead, and pretended sanctity of life? All these, I think, should be really practiced by us.
>
> It is not sufficient for you alone to be blameless. Entreat or compel all the priests that are in Galatia to be virtuous, too. If they and their wives, children, and servants do not attend the worship of the gods, expel them from the priestly function. And also forbear to converse with the servants, children, and wives of the Galileans, who are impious towards the gods, and prefer impiety to religion. Admonish also every priest not to frequent the theater, nor to drink in taverns, nor to exercise any trade or employment that is mean and

disgraceful. Those who obey you, honor; and those who disobey you, expel.

Where have we heard instructions like these before? Oh—it was from Hippolytus, telling us that Christians couldn't have anything to do with shameful professions like the theater, which had its beginnings as a pagan religious rite.

But it's not enough that the priests should be good examples. Christians get all the credit for taking care of the poor. Pagans should have a piece of that racket, too.

Put up hostels in every city, too, so that strangers may share our benevolence; and not only those of our own religion, but, if they are indigent, others also.

Hostels! Where did Julian get an idea like that? Could it have been from Basil of Caesarea, who was Julian's old school chum, and whose "new city" was a new wonder of the world?

But building programs and charitable foundations is expensive. Christians are used to giving large gifts to pay for all their charity. The only way Julian can see it working for the pagans, though, is if he has the provincial government pay for it.

How these expenses are to be defrayed must now be considered. I have ordered Galatia to supply you with thirty thousand bushels of wheat every year, of which the fifth part is to be given to the poor who attend on the priests, and the remainder to be distributed among strangers and our own beggars. For when none of the Jews beg, and the impious Galileans relieve both their own poor and ours, it is shameful that ours should be destitute of our assistance.

Here is the admission that makes this passage famous. No matter how much he hates the Christians, Julian has to concede that they take care of the poor— not just Christian poor, but anyone who needs help. And it's *obvious* to him that this is a good thing. It wouldn't have been obvious to earlier generations of pagans, but it's obvious to Julian.

Julian will have the state kick-start his charity program, but he's hoping that the pagans will start to act more like Christians once they see it working.

Therefore, teach the Hellenists [Julian's term for the pagans] to contribute to such ministerial functions, and the Hellenic villages to offer to the gods their first-fruits.[59]

Obviously, if they have to be taught, this isn't a thing the pagans have been doing. Christians bring their first fruits to the altar as part of their worship. Jews do it, too. But pagans—well, maybe they did once upon a time, but they're going to have to learn from scratch.

In another letter to a priest, Julian sees Christian charity as a sort of conspiracy:

---

59 Julian, *Letter to Arsacius*, translated by John Duncombe (altered).

For when it came about that the poor were neglected and overlooked by the priests, then I think the impious Galileans observed this fact and devoted themselves to philanthropy. And they have gained ascendancy in the worst of their deeds through the credit they win for such practices.[60]

They can't get away with it, Julian says. We'll be just as charitable as they are, and our priests will be even more virtuous.

Wilmer Cave Wright, who edited the Loeb edition of Julian's works, pointed out that Julian was saying things here that had never been said by pagans in the good old days. Wright couldn't account for Julian's ideas except by saying that he'd taken them from the hated Galileans.

He saw that in order to offset the influence of the Christian priests, which he thought was partly due to their moral teaching, partly to their charity towards the poor, the pagans must follow their example. Hitherto the preaching of morals had been left to the philosophers. Julian's admonitions as to the treatment of the poor and those in prison, and the rules that he lays down for the private life of a priest, are evidently borrowed from the Christians.[61]

---

60 Julian, *Fragment of a Letter to a Pagan Priest* 305B, translated by Wilmer Cave Wright, altered.
61 Wright (editor), *The Works of the Emperor Julian*, Vol. 2, 295.

It may be true to say that Julian's program for a pagan church was "borrowed" from the Christians, but that's not all that's going on here. It would be better to say that Christianity had already changed the world. It was *self-evidently true* to Julian that these things ought to be done. The poor ought to be taken care of. The priests ought to stay away from scandalous plays and vice-ridden taverns. And it never occurred to Julian that these things had never been true in the pagan world he thought he wanted to go back to. They hadn't been true because no one had thought they were good things until the Christians came along.

Here's Julian in another part of the same letter, telling his priest how a good pagan shares his material goods.

> Now, we ought to share our goods with all people—but more freely with the just, on the one hand, and on the other with the helpless and poor. But I will say, even if it is speaking a paradox, that even with the wicked we ought to share clothes and food: for we give to the humanity, not to the manners.[62]

What pagan would ever have said something like that? We ought to share our goods with the *wicked*? If there really were a Zeus, he'd be getting a thunderbolt ready.

---

62 Julian, *Fragment of a Letter to a Priest* 290D (new translation).

No, Julian was a Christian through and through, no matter how much he hated the name of "Galilean." His whole thought had been formed in a world where the Christian revolution had already happened. And his problem with the Christians of his time was that they weren't Christian *enough*. He wanted to return to a golden age when pagans took care of the poor and lived sober and blameless lives—but that golden age never existed, except in Julian's completely Christianized imagination.

It had only been half a century since Constantine made Christianity legal. Now it was hard even for a pagan to avoid thinking like a Christian. The Christian idea of charity changed the world, even for the people who weren't Christian.

I think Julian knew that something was missing in his scheme. He knew he'd have to make the government pay for his pagan charities, because he didn't have the Mass.

For all the early Christian writers, the Mass was the beginning of charity. It was the source of charity. It was a mingling of our perishable flesh with Jesus's immortal flesh, and so a mingling of divine life with our own. The Mass was what empowered Christians to be Christ to the world—to bring it healing, consolation, friendship, and relief of its suffering.

Here's the way the great liturgical scholar Virgil Michel put it in the middle of the twentieth century:

> What the early Christians . . . did at the altar of God, in the central act of Christian worship, they also lived out in their daily lives. They understood fully that the common action of their worship was to be the inspiration of all their actions. They knew well that they common giving of themselves to God and to the brethren of Christ was in fact a solemn promise made to God that they would live their lives in this same love of God and of God's children, their brethren in Christ, throughout all the day. Unless they did that, their action before God's altar would be at best lip-service, a lie before God.[63]

Father Michel was simply observing what is evident in all the pages of the Fathers' writings. A third-century manual of Church discipline, for example, tells its readers that "widows and orphans are to be revered like the altar."

Such a command envisions a social life based on a network of charity, but it presumes a deep, deep Eucharistic piety. It presumes an altar that is revered and beloved, because it belongs to Jesus.

It's a social life based on the inner transformation of persons. Those who received Holy Communion were held accountable to the life of Christ—just as St. Paul had held the Corinthians accountable.

We're still held accountable today.

---

63 Virgil Michel, "The Cooperative Movement and the Liturgical Movement," in *Orate Fratres* 14, no. 4 (1940).

But we're held accountable by love, not by accountants. Once you have that gift, once you really discern the body (see 1 Corinthians 11:29), you *have* to go out and share it. It's not because anyone is keeping tabs on you. It's not because there was a ledger with your acts of charity registered in it at the deacon's office in your parish.

No, it's because the Eucharist has filled you with Christ's love—filled you to overflowing. The love has to go *somewhere*.

And there's a whole world out there that desperately needs it.

Conclusion

WORK, PLAY, AND LOVE

It's all about the Mass.

Work is a good thing. It was meant to be a joy: God placed Adam and Eve in Eden to work, to be his partners in the business of creation. And work still can be a joy, when we realize that work is part of our Christian mission. Our work is our offering at the one altar for the whole world. All the things we do to support ourselves are made holy at the altar when we bring them forward—figuratively or literally—with the offering. And when we receive the Eucharist, God is giving us the power we need to go out and do *his* work, to collaborate with him in creation.

It's all about the Mass.

Even in a perfect world, we were meant to have time off. Play is a holy thing. We don't just take time off so we can have the energy to get back to work. We do it because, from the moment of creation, we were meant to be creatures who did more than just support ourselves. We were meant to be like God in our work and our rest. God loved us so much that he wanted to share the Sabbath with us. He wanted us to take time to contemplate the goodness of his creation—the creation our work cooperated in.

IT'S ALL ABOUT THE MASS.

When we encounter the love of God face-to-face in the Eucharist, we can't help taking that love out with us. We understand why we worked so hard, and why we had to take time off from working to worship. It's because of love. Love radiates out from the Eucharist and changes the world.

THE EARLY CHRISTIANS knew the Mass to be their bond. This is evident throughout the Holy Scriptures.

It's foreshadowed in the Old Testament, in the sacrifice of Melchizedek, offered on behalf of Abraham—a sacrifice of bread and wine.

It's foreshadowed in the manna that sustained Israel in the desert.

It's foreshadowed in the Bread of the Presence in Jerusalem's Temple.

In the New Testament it's foreshadowed in Jesus's multiplication of loaves. What love he had for the hungry and the poor!

But all those foreshadowings are *fulfilled* at the Last Supper, when all the love of God, all the divine charity, was poured into common bread and wine.

And now we see the love played out in the life of the Church.

Or at least we *should*.

Divine communion leads us to deeper communion with one another. Or rather it *should* lead us to deeper communion with one another. It should make us a people bound together by charity. By love. But it's hard for me—and probably for you, too—to spend five minutes on social media without wondering whether we're failing in the way we live up to the powerful social bond that God gives us so freely in Holy Communion.

We are, of course, not the first Christians to live in divisive times. The saints in every age have had to be countercultural. The saints in every age, in fact, have found their remedy to social unrest in the Mass.

The Holy Mass was serious business for those early Christians. They held themselves accountable to it every day.

Every day they knew they were living off their last Communion. Every day they knew they were living toward their next Communion.

Thus the Mass had everyday application. It went with a Christian to work, to the market, to the kitchen, to the bedroom. Everything a Christian did in all those places was united with the sacrifice placed upon the altar—the fruit of the earth and the work of human hands.

And so the Mass had profound social implications. And it has implications just as profound today.

This is what the Fathers knew: The kingdom of Christ has arrived, because Jesus reigns now in the Blessed Sacrament of the altar. Jesus reigns in the Church. That is the constant teaching of the early Fathers.

The Eucharist empowers Christians in every age to build up new cultures on the ruins of the old ones. As the old Roman Empire crumbled there arose a new world order, with new institutions—hospitals and universities, soup kitchens and homeless shelters, hospices and hostels. A "culture of death" crumbled, and in its place Christians were able to begin a civilization of love.

The Mass does not *force* us to do this. But if we know what we're about, we'll feel compelled to take Christ's love into the streets. It's one of the great paradoxes of Christian life that we cannot keep faith, we cannot keep hope, and we cannot keep love unless we give them away. Unless we evangelize. Unless we live charity. Unless we love sacrificially.

This doesn't mean we'll be appreciated. All the most refined Roman philosophers found the Christians loathsome. The historian Tacitus said the Christians deserved to die. And the philosopher-emperor Marcus Aurelius agreed. The emperor Nero could succeed at convicting the Christians of a crime called "hatred of humanity." People were willing to believe that Christian love was really a cover for deep-seated hatred.

Can you imagine a society where devout Christians are called haters?

Christian love will seem repugnant to those who are mired in sin. They cannot see love at first. They must gradually adjust their eyes to the light. But if we don't give up, and if we persist in loving them, they may one day see our love for what it is. They may one day see the gift and accept it. They may one day join us at the altar.

St. Augustine said it most succinctly: Those who see charity have seen the Trinity.

Through the Eucharist God changes us into himself—as surely as he changed the elements of bread and wine. He forms us as living stones in the temple of his Church. He builds up a Eucharistic culture to replace the culture of death.

He has done this before, in the lives of the Fathers, in the world of the Roman Empire, where the culture of death had gone further than any of us have ever seen it in our lifetimes. He will do it again with us, in our land, in our time.

Did I mention this? It's all about the Mass.

Acknowledgments

The English translations I used for this book were mostly completed in the nineteenth century (and a few before that). In some cases I have adapted them to reflect twenty-first-century usage. I make a full confession of this in the footnotes.

I want to thank two friends whose conversation helped me to develop the ideas in this book. Joseph T. Stuart, the great scholar of Christopher Dawson, sent me to the sources most illuminating for my introduction. Christopher Bailey, my multilingual neighbor, produced new translations when I needed them. I'm useless without my friends, and I don't hesitate to credit them for the good I do. All the mistakes herein are mine alone.

Bibliography

1. Original sources

Abbreviations:

ANCL: *Ante-Nicene Christian Library*.

ANF: *Ante-Nicene Fathers*.

CCC: *Catechism of the Catholic Church*.

NPNF: *Nicene and Post-Nicene Fathers*.

The Apostolical Constitutions: or, Canons of the Apostles, in Coptic. With an English translation by Henry Tattam. London: Oriental Translation Fund, 1848.

Aristotle. *The Nicomachean Ethics of Aristotle*. Translated by R. W. Browne. London: George Bell and Sons, 1889.

Aristotle. *Politics*, in *Aristotle's Ethics and Politics, Comprising his Practical Philosophy*. Trans. by John Gillies. London: T. Cadell and W. Davies, 1813.

Aulus Gellius. *The Attic Nights of Aulus Gellius*. Trans. by the Rev. W. Beloe. London: J. Johnson, 1795.

Ausonius. *Ausonius*, with an English translation by Hugh G. Evelyn White. London: William Heinemann, 1919.

Hippolytus. *The Treatise on the Apostolic Tradition of St Hippolytus of Rome, Bishop and Martyr*. Edited by the Rev. Gregory Dix. London: Society for Promoting Christian Knowledge, 1937.

Julian the Apostate. *Select Works of the Emperor Julian, And Some Pieces of the Sophist Libanius.* Trans. by John Duncombe. London: J. Nichols, 1784.

The Works of the Emperor Julian. Ed. and trans. by Wilmer Cave Wright. London: William Heinemann, 1913–1923 (3 volumes).

Juvenal. *The Satyrs of Decimus Junius Juvenalus, and of Aulus Persius Flaccus.* Translated into English verse by Mr. Dryden, and several other eminent hands. London: J. Tonson, 1726.

Plautus. *M. Accius Plautus ex fide atque auctoritate complurium librorum manuscriptorum opera Dionys. Lambini Monstroliensis emendatus.* Paris: Apud Ioannem Macaeum, 1577.

Pliny the Younger. *The Letters of Pliny the Consul.* Trans. by William Melmoth. London: Lackington, Allen, & Co., 1802.

Xenophon. *Memoirs of Socrates. With the Defense of Socrates Before His Judges.* Translated from the original Greek by Sarah Fielding. Bath (England): C. Pope, 1762.

2. Secondary sources

Augustine of Hippo, St. *Sermons* 336.1, *Patrologia Latina* 38, 1472.

Brown, Peter. *Through the Eye of a Needle.* Princeton, NJ: Princeton University Press, 2012.

Dawson, Christopher. *Religion and the Rise of Culture.* Washington, DC: Catholic University Press, 2013.

Dobson, William T. *Literary Frivolities, Fancies, Follies and Frolics*. London: Chatto and Windus, 1880.

Gregory of Nazianzus, "Body and Soul." Trans. Elizabeth Barrett Browning, in *The Complete Works of Mrs. E. B. Browning*, vol. VI (New York: George D. Sproul, 1901), 192.

Hamman, Andre. *The Mass: Ancient Liturgies and Patristic Texts*. Staten Island, NY: Alba House, 1967.

Heschel, Abraham Joshua. *The Sabbath: Its Meaning for Modern Man*. New York: Farrar Straus Giroux, 1990.

Heyne, Thomas. "Reconstructing the World's First Hospital: the Basiliad." In *Hektoen International: A Journal of Medical Humanities*, online at https://hekint .org/2017/02/24/reconstructing-the-worlds-first -hospital-the-basiliad.

Holman, Susan R. (editor). *Wealth and Poverty in Early Church and Society*. Grand Rapids, MI: Baker Academic, 2008.

Hopkins, Gerard Manley. *A Selection of His Poems and Prose*. Baltimore: Penguin, 1953, 27.

Jungmann, Josef A., S.J. *Handing on the Faith: A Manual of Catechetics*. New York: Herder and Herder, 1962.

Michel, Virgil. "The Cooperative Movement and the Liturgical Movement." *Orate Fratres* 14, no. 4 (1940).

Murphy-O'Connor, Jerome. *St. Paul's Corinth*. Collegeville, MN. The Liturgical Press, 2002.

Pieper, Joseph. *Leisure the Basis of Culture*. New York: Mentor-Omega, 1963.

Roberts, Michael. *The Jeweled Style: Poetry and Poetics in Late Antiquity.* Ithaca, NY: Cornell University Press, 1989.

Smith, Dennis E. *From Symposium to Eucharist.* Minneapolis Fortress Press, 2003.

Uhlhorn, Gerhard: *Christian Charity in the Ancient Church.* New York: Charles Scribner's Sons, 1883.

Veyne, Paul (editor). *A History of Private Life, Vol. I: From Pagan Rome to Byzantium.* Cambridge, MA: Belknap Press, 1986.

Volz, Carl A. "Lex Orandi, Lex Operandi: The Relationship of Worship and Work in the Early Church" (1987). Valparaiso, IN: Institute of Liturgical Studies Occasional Papers, 28.

About the Author

 MIKE AQUILINA is author of more than fifty books, including *The Fathers of the Church*, *The Mass of the Early Christians*, and *A Year with the Church Fathers*. He has co-hosted eleven series that air on the Eternal Word Television Network (EWTN). He has co-authored books with contemporary Christian music pioneer John Michael Talbot and theologian Scott Hahn. He is past editor of *New Covenant* magazine and *The Pittsburgh Catholic* newspaper. He appears weekly on Sirius Radio's *Sonrise Morning Show*. Mike and his wife, Terri, have six children, who are the subject of his book *Love in the Little Things*.

In 2011 Mike was a featured presenter of the U.S. Bishops' Diocesan Educational/Catechetical Leadership Institute. He also wrote the USCCB's theological reflection for Catechetical Sunday in 2011.

His reviews, essays, and journalism have appeared in many journals, including *First Things*, *Touchstone*, *Crisis*, *Our Sunday Visitor*, *National Catholic Register*, and *Catholic Heritage*. He contributed work on early Christianity to the *Encyclopedia of Catholic Social Thought*.

Mike is also a poet whose works have appeared in U.S. literary journals and have been translated into Polish and Spanish. He writes music with Rock and Roll Hall of Fame artist Dion DiMucci, and his songs have been recorded and performed by Dion, Paul Simon, Christy Altomare, and others.

You may also be interested in . . .

Saints at Heart
Bert Ghezzi
ISBN 978-1-64060-203-8
$14.99
Trade Paperback

The Illumined Heart
Frederica Mathewes-Green
ISBN 978-1-55725-553-2
$18.99